FORCED
to FLY

*An anthology of writings that will make
you see the funny side of living abroad*

by Expatriates Everywhere

Second Edition

SUMMERTIME PUBLISHING

First Published edition published 1998
by Summertime Publishing

Second edition published 2012 by Summertime Publishing
© Copyright Forced to Fly, Jo Parfitt
© Copyright of each individual piece remains with its author

ISBN: 978-1-904881-41-4

Proofread by Shelley Antscherl

With thanks to Alexandra Weston Moffett for editorial
assistance.

Cover design www.creationbooth.com

Internal illustrations and layout Alison Day Designs:
www.alisonday.nl

CONTENTS

FOREWORD

PART ONE

PART TWO

Departures

FOREWORD

The ink was barely dry when I read the original edition of *Forced to Fly* after meeting author Jo Parfitt — for the first time! — at a conference about mobile women and families in Paris back in 1998. Quietly whispering in my ear about her book during a session, I remember the word humour above all else that she said to me on that day.

Using humour has always been my own trademark when it comes to discussing matters of international mobility. It disarms and distracts people from their insecurities and fears. Indeed, retaining your sense of humour is one of the first rules of relocation, especially an international move. So, I knew even before opening its original pages that I was going to relish reading the collection of other people's stories about becoming a global citizen. I think I even whispered back to Jo that as I had a terrible fear of flying, perhaps I could write a story and call it *Forced to Fly Far*.

Our giggling, at that point, likely got us both tossed from the conference session. It was worth it though for both the friendship and over a decade of collaboration on expat book projects and lectures which followed.

Writing a new series of books soon after our first meeting (on one of which Jo herself served as editor), I got distracted. But I have faithfully devoured everything she has produced in the intervening years — too many books to count. All of them written with the same care and dedication to helping expat women find themselves in the experiences of others. And, often as not, laugh about it.

Forced to Fly came out near the beginning of Jo's long and distinguished writing and publishing career assisting expat spouses so is therefore special. That she has decided to bring it back into print, expanded, with even more funny stories, should help calm down everyone who reads it. Whether it's chuckling over a bad hair cut in a foreign country (an experience every woman can relate to) or entertaining visitors one may not even know but are friends of friends of friends, there is at least one story and likely many more within these pages that expat readers will savour.

Have a giggle. And enjoy.

Robin Pascoe

Author of *Homeward Bound, Raising Global Nomads, Moveable Marriage* and *A Broad Abroad.*

All published by Expatriate Press.

PART ONE

Coping With Culture Shock
Linda March

Linda was on the move for most of her childhood. When, at last, she thought she had settled down in England, her family was posted to Norway.

For the first time in my life I felt truly at home. After a nomadic childhood and then moves associated with university, jobs, career changes and marriage, I was now firmly rooted in the place I wanted to be: a Victorian home which was finally just the way we wanted, only 10 minutes from the seafront.

Our two little girls were happily settled in the school at which I had until recently been teaching. Many of the staff were personal friends and had known my girls since they'd seen the first twinkle in my eye and bulge in my waistband. I had a doctor who knew my name and who had been there for both deliveries. After years of nightmare experiences, I had found the best dentist in the world and if I ever had a bad hair day then an appointment with Helen could fix it. My weekly shopping at Waitrose took half the morning because the aisles were an obstacle course of people from church, ex-colleagues, mothers of children I had taught and, of course, friends who could tempt me out of the morning's plans and into the coffee shop. I knew the short cuts to avoid the traffic from here to there across town and, most importantly, I knew where everything and everyone was — where to look for a widget, where to find out about ballet lessons, the best child-friendly restaurants, whom to call when the house was suddenly and inexplicably invaded by flying insects. So, yes, for the first time in my life I felt truly settled. Then, if you've picked up this book you will guess what happened — I was forced to fly to Norway as a trailing spouse (although I was at that time thankfully unaware of my unflattering new title).

To tell the truth I was a bit miffed. To tell the real truth I was beside myself with rage! Furious with my husband for 'making' us go, 'making' us leave our lovely home for some horrible cold place miles from here, despite his constant offers to turn the job down if it was going to make me this unhappy; resenting his company for making him an offer that was too good to turn down; afraid of how I would cope in a strange environment; deeply saddened at leaving old friends and family and heartbroken at the prospect of wrenching my daughters from their nearby beloved grandmother.

And so the nightmare began. For weeks the walls of our home reverberated with yells or pure silence as we alternated between fighting and not speaking. Then John departed to find a house for us and an office for the new Norwegian branch of his company and so, with a heavy heart, a churning stomach and a feeling that I was powerless to control my fate, I organised the million and one things that have to be done before beginning an international move — sorting out, throwing out, crying, packing up, informing the world and his wife of our unpronounceable new address, crying, finding tenants for my lovely home, crying and saying endless goodbyes.

The 360 mile drive to Newcastle in high winds with a tarpaulin flying free as the rope holding it in place over the roof rack luggage worked loose and necessitated stops every few miles, was conducted mostly in tears. The 19 hour ferry crossing in the same high winds was spent mostly with my head in a sick bag, perversely grateful that the girls were also sick; otherwise I would never have coped had they wanted to leave the cabin. John had offered to meet us at Stavanger harbour, but as our new home was apparently only 10 minutes away, and as the car was stacked to the gunwales with everything we might need to make us, and particularly the children, feel at home until our shipment arrived, I'd told him not to bother. I'd blithely asked him just to give me directions — I was bound to be able to find it — I'd managed the first million miles of the journey without help, I was pretty sure I could manage the last seven kilometres.

And if I thought the nightmare had begun, well I was really in for a shock. John's new position of setting up an office in Norway meant that we were completely alone. There was no big company, foreign service or military organisation behind us. We had no one to show us the ropes, invite us for coffee and thrust a welcome pack in our hands. We were on our own and although Norway is not, on the surface, so culturally different from the UK, and despite the fact that so many Norwegians speak excellent English, as complete strangers we just didn't know where to begin. Nine days after our arrival John went offshore to work and, if three months previously I had felt truly settled for the first time in my life, now I felt truly abandoned for the first time in my life, particularly as a nagging stomach pain grew worse and worse. Two days later I found myself in a foreign hospital suffering from excruciatingly painful kidney stones (read Sick in Stavanger later in this book). Fifteen months later sitting in one of our favourite restaurants in Stavanger with my mother, who was on one of her regular visits, the girls broke off from their excited description of their previous weekend's skiing trip and their insistence that Grandma should come to see them ice skating the next day, to wave to school friends who had just walked in. As I confidently translated the menu for her, my mother suddenly exclaimed proudly, "You've done it, Linda, you've made a new life for your family." I gazed out at the familiar harbour and felt a surge of pride too. Yes, I had done it, but the journey from the hospital to the restaurant was a long one, via a deep dark tunnel that began with severe culture shock and ended with successful coping strategies.

Culture Shock: What is it?

In *Moving and Living Abroad,* Albright, Cho and Austin identify the 'typical expatriate morale curve'. They suggest that the pre-departure and very early arrival stage is often a peak honeymoon period, characterised by 'enthusiasm, sociability and self-confidence — and ignorance of real cultural differences'. This is followed by the trough of despair, a time when you start to hate everything and everyone. This is true culture shock. You feel alone, ostracised even, and this can last for weeks, or months, until signs of adaptation and peaks of contentment appear. This final stage, when you can at last leave behind the limbo of transition, is called integration. Although stressful periods can occur at any time during an overseas assignment, it is generally agreed that the period of maximum stress usually occurs in the first year.

Oh dear, so culture shock really exists. Does that mean we all have to take a ride on this emotional roller coaster every time we face a location move? I'm afraid so, but let's be positive, there may be low spots but there are also highs. And one important thought to hold on to when you're hurtling down into the depths of culture shock is that others have hurtled as you are hurtling now. They have felt what you are feeling and they understand. You are not weak, inadequate, pathetic or going round the twist. You are passing through a phase we all have to go through and like the terrible twos and teenage pimples, it's a phase you will leave behind. The light at the end of the tunnel is, in the findings of Albright, Cho and Austin, that '[Culture shock] is a profound learning experience, which can lead to a great degree of self-awareness and personal growth. The growth may take time and may be painful, but the results are usually worth it'. In my opinion they are well worth it.

I'm pleased to hear that many people experience a honeymoon period on arrival in their new location. My strong negative attitude to moving meant that I went straight to jail without collecting £200 — straight to that time when the honeymoon's over, when culture shock steps in. Culture shock is a very personal experience. For me, it manifested itself in the million different ways in which everything was different.

To the friendly outgoing Texan, whose back garden gate opened onto a well worn path around the beautiful Norwegian fjord, culture shock was wrapped up in the way Norwegians walked stonily past without an acknowledgement, far less a cheery smile.

To the British mother of two young boys, at her wit's end during a cold, rainy half term holiday who telephoned the local Tourist office to find out if any children's activities were laid on that week, it was being told to take them shopping because some of the shops had Lego tables.

Your new home may be a hotel; a tiny flat in an inhospitable block assigned to aliens; it may be surrounded by armed guards; it may be bigger and better than the one you've come from. In some foreign postings it may even contain servants who attend to your every need, but whatever it is, it isn't home — at least not yet. You're in the grip of culture shock because everything is different and everyone is different. If you just go over the hill or round the corner you won't see a familiar landmark and get your bearings. That tall red headed figure you caught sight of out of the corner of your eye isn't your best friend. Your heart sinks at the realisation that there's no one to laugh with about that awful incident in the supermarket this morning: your attempt to peek and discover whether the bag that held, what felt and sounded like oats actually contained oats, resulted in a splitting-sound and a floor strewn with split peas.

Just moving to a new location in your own country where you understand the language and culture is difficult enough — you know you need to go to Boots the Chemist, but you still have to find where Boots is, but it's even harder when everything around you is strange and there's no Boots to go to. And in very foreign locations your senses may be assailed by different smells, sounds, light and colours. However, the foreignness of the location is not always an indication of the level of culture shock.

One British multi-mover remarked that despite having lived in the very different and austere locations of Russia and Azerbaijan, she suffered more culture shock in locations closer to home, like France and Norway, simply because others expected that she would instantly cope and so no one offered help. In far flung locations the expatriate network is usually highly developed.

Every day has a million problems and the local equivalent of the Yellow Pages telephone directory doesn't hold the answer to it. What is the Norwegian/Thai/Spanish/Russian for hairdresser/exhaust fitter/urine infection/sultanas? Everyday tasks take forever, and how, and where do you do them? How do you feed your finicky family with unrecognisable cuts of meat, a limited or bizarre choice of vegetables and fruit that costs four times as much as it would at home? You find yourself carrying about your own desert island as you tune out of the world around you because you can't understand conversations, signs, headlines, radio. And, on a day when you can't find the chicken stock cubes and resort, exhausted to accosting a cashier and doing an impersonation of a chicken while drawing a square box on the back of an envelope, it can tip you over the edge.

And of course, everyone else is doing just fine. Your new world is peopled with confident, coping, outgoing women for whom moving from one side of the world to another is just a breeze. They all have wonderful social lives, successful children (well, they would have: they're all perfect mothers) and hundreds of friends. At least that's the way it seems to you. They seem to be laughing down at you from the top of the mountain. You, meanwhile, are stuck on the starting slopes. Anyway, they're not your sort. And so isolation begins.

Homesickness

Well, of course, everything at home was better. Everyone at home was better. You don't want any new friends, you want your old ones. It goes without saying how much you miss the company of friends and family, but it can be quite surprising to discover just how much you miss acquaintances and places. I inexplicably missed the enterprising young lad who used to sell and deliver my bin bags and who always had a tale to tell of his girlfriend and his daughter on his fortnightly appearances at my door. And there's another thing, as one woman in the throes of homesickness remarked, "The door bell never rings and I never open the door to find a friend standing there."

Transition and Coping with Change

It makes sense to try and be as prepared as possible for your new location and your new life — doing your homework in advance, having a contact to call on, psyching up your children, maybe taking a pre-move reconnaissance trip, but however prepared you are you will still have to go through the transition of really saying goodbye to one place and being in another. From the first news that you are moving until you are sitting in that favourite restaurant, you are in limbo. Limbo and transition are lengthy and painful, but take heart, where there are endings there are also beginnings.

If easy things like buying bread are hard to cope with in your new location, then hard things are even harder to cope with. Moving to a new location is a significant change in our lives, but other changes are happening all the time too. Most multi-movers are moving around at stages in their lives when there are many other important changes: career changes for themselves or their partner, the birth of children, new schools, illness or even death of relatives far away back home.

Katherine Prendergast, an American psychotherapist working on a Family Crisis Intervention Team and herself an international mover, has seen the following phenomena many, many times.

"Crises, life changes or transitions seem to come in groups of three — almost a ripple effect. Most of us handle the first crisis and even the second relatively well. But it is the third crisis which seems to put us over the edge. We have used up our emotional and physical energy and strength dealing with the first two crises — there's little left for the third. This is when we need the help and support of our family, friends and professionals to help us cope and successfully move on," Katherine explains.

In a new location family and friends aren't there and you have no idea where to go for professional help when you can't speak the language or understand how the health system works.

Making a New Life

Let's face it, as a trailing spouse, you're the one who is going to have to do it. The likelihood is that your partner will just swap one office for another with the same company logo, same computer system, and only a lighter or heavier weight suit to deal with (poor darling). If a real new life is to be built then you are going to have to lay the foundation stones — but they can be heavy bricks to carry so give yourself time. It's okay to have a bad day, a bad week, a bad month, but it's not okay to hibernate forever. Be gentle with yourself as you would with your children, feel sorry for yourself — you've had a hard day discovering that self raising flour doesn't exist here, the oven is useless and that your best recipe cake that is guaranteed to cheer everyone up has hardened into a piece of local granite. But, just as after a reasonable amount of time you would coax a recalcitrant youngster out of his room, coax yourself out into the world. It's time to kill your time, to make friends, to get involved.

Ask for Help

If you need help — and you are going to need help — then ask for it. If you're on your own without the safety net of a large organisation then ask a friendly mum who said 'hello' in the school playground. The odds are that she's a recovering culture shock victim, will remember what it's like and help; and if she doesn't then ask someone else. Keep asking — you'll probably get the chance to return the favour before too long.

When I slid on a pool of water in the bathroom and heard the crack of my ankle bone, I just knew I was going to need help. Over the next two months, as I worked my way back to mobility, the contents of my kitchen cupboards became as familiar to the mothers of my children's classmates as my children became to the insides of their cars. Like Tennessee Williams' Blanche, I had to rely on the kindness of strangers and their kindness overwhelmed me. Most of my 'thank you's' were met with, "Well, it could happen to any of us, we're all in the same boat with no old friends and family to call on."

Say Yes

The advice of another much more mobile wife and mother who seemed to adjust remarkably quickly to her new surroundings was, "accept any invitations offered". And when they're offered, fix a date and time, don't leave it hanging vaguely in mid-air, you'll lose the impetus or courage and never get around to ringing. Don't wait too long to take that step towards friendship.

Conventional behaviour at home might make you wait several months or even years before developing a friendship — nodding at the gate for three months, progressing to 'Good morning' for another three and then eventually asking how the children are. In this way it can be years before you move on to real friendship or an invitation to dinner. In your new life your fellow friendly expat will have moved on to pastures new in that time and you may have missed the chance of a beautiful friendship. It's sad if you find out at their leaving party that you had so much in common and could have been good friends, so don't let the grass grow under your feet.

There's no two ways about it: unless you are a complete loner, then to be tolerably happy you are going to have to make friends. One way to do that is to accept all invitations.

But what if none come? Then you have to make the moves. However, if the thought of hoving up to a room or playground of complete strangers, whose only connection with you is that they come from the same country or have children in the same class as yours, and saying a cheery, "Hi everyone, I'm Linda!" fills you with horror, then find more natural ways to get to know people. The old ones are the best: join groups, societies, sign up to help sew the costumes for the school Christmas play. An offer of help works wonders and gives you a purpose to be there, a role, a natural way to relate to others. Accept everything — if you end up doing too much at least you'll be busy and the phone will ring. You can always offload when you've had time to work out what you really want to spend your time doing.

Being forced out of your safe, cosy routine is scary. It can be traumatic to face 7.30 on a Monday evening without *Coronation Street* after a lifetime of its companionship, but the change will make you shake yourself up. Maybe there's something else you could do that you've never thought of. Now is the time to try.

Children

The good news is that so called 'Third Culture Kids' — born in one country, moved to another, and calling yet another home — are the citizens who will fit into the 21st century's mobile world. The bad news is that, like you, they may have to go through that deep dark tunnel to get there. The worse news is that you may have to put up with tantrums, bad dreams and bed wetting on the journey. Different ages will, of course, have different problems — teenagers, for whom fitting in is vital, will probably refuse to go without giving you hell. Little ones may react to the upheaval by refusing to let you out of their sight. Accept your children and their reactions. Remember that you are the constant in their lives and try to create as much stability as possible. Prepare them for the changes and keep the channels of communication open. Help create memories for them.

Much-moved Carlanne Herzog, who is a professional Cultural Trainer, advises photographing the real places you see and use everyday — the school playground, the grocery shop. We tend to take our cameras on the once in a lifetime trips up mountains, rivers or monuments. But the places we and our children will really want to be reminded of are the everyday places that made up our lives in this location.

I recently met Joanna, a five-year-old who had moved to Singapore from Jakarta for a month during the troubles. When we met she was on summer holiday in England. She asked if I would like to see her 'school book' from Singapore and showed me a simple A4 sheaf of stapled papers. Her class teacher had pasted photographs of the pupils and the daily routines and photocopied them. 'This is where we wash our hands after 'play time' and 'first we put our reading folders in Miss White's basket' and so on were among the descriptions. To Joanna this book was vitally important and provided a link to her current reality.

Remember that it's as important for your child to say his or her goodbyes as it is for you. Why not let your child hand out pre-addressed, pre-stamped postcards to his school friends? In that way he is sure to be remembered for a while.

Let your child know a little of how you are feeling. Don't be too over enthusiastic about your new location. Children need to know that it is okay to express their emotions. If you show you are sad, they can be sad too.

Visitors and Home Visits

Your new location may be glamorous, sunny, and warm — the ideal holiday spot. Before you leave you say, "Come and see us" and people that you previously would spend an evening with now blow their life savings to travel half way round the world to spend two weeks holiday with you, and you had never realised just how awful their children were. Your visitors often assume that because they are on holiday you are on holiday.

This is not necessarily the case. You may be trying to keep piano lessons, Brownies and homework going in between, acting as a local guide, gourmet cook and wine drinker extraordinaire. And, you still have to get up at the crack of dawn to fill lunch boxes and do the school run, A service wife stationed at a particularly desirable holiday location recalls one incoming batch of visitors spending their first night on the floor while they waited for the previous batch to depart; her life, when she wasn't at her full time job, was a whirl of sheet changing and laundry.

Visitors are wonderful, especially in the early days. A friendly face from home to explore your new location with and to really talk to is a real joy. But living in each other's pockets for too long can add a strain. Be aware and learn to take a deep breath. Help your visitors to be as independent as possible so that they can take themselves off to see the local 'must' of a tourist site. There's a limit to how many times you can 'ooh' and 'aah' at the same relic.

The stress of too many people cooped up together in the same house can also arise on home visits. An answer may be to rent a holiday home and hire a car for the duration. This gives you the freedom of your own base and own mobility and the option to invite people to come to you instead of spending your entire home leave on the motorway from friends to parents to distant uncles. It also enables your children to react to their reverse culture shock like complete brats without it being constantly on display to others.

A Few More Don'ts for Home Visits

Don't go home too soon, it can be very unsettling and your return journey can drop you right back into those uncomfortable first feelings of culture shock.

And, in my opinion, avoid the unspeakable madness of travelling half way round the world alone with small children. If your spouse really, truly can't travel with you then he should either be shot at dawn or prepared to shell out for someone to accompany you. An American expatriate wife faced with undertaking the long haul and three changes of aircraft between Stavanger and New Orleans alone, just knew she would lose one of her three youngsters in an airport, so offered her sister an expenses paid holiday in beautiful Norway providing she undertook the return journey with them.

Once home try and avoid the even greater madness of buying everything in sight. On my first trip home I almost burst into tears in the Waitrose supermarket. Such clearly, cleanly, beautifully laid out goods, such choice, such prices! I felt as if I was in Aladdin's cave and wanted to buy everything. Similar feelings are aroused in many familiar stores. Whether you are arriving home from an extremely expensive country, so that everything at home is half the price, or from a country where you just cannot get the goods you need, take a deep breath before you buy too many things that just 'might come in handy'. They just might not and will be a headache to get rid of when you're clearing out for your next move in two years' time.

Reverse Culture Shock

Your return home, either for a visit or for repatriation, can throw you into reverse culture shock. You have to learn to live with your own people again, people who don't have your newly acquired breadth of experience.

Homecoming expectations can cause another large peak as the assignment comes to an end (that is if you are, by then, happy to be going home), but the thrill of repatriation is often countered by the realism of friends and relatives who are uninterested in your experience. You may find a new job that does not take advantage of your new skills, if you can find a job at all. You may find that your confidence takes a hammering too.

Carlanne Herzog, whose training courses include the tellingly titled, *So you think you're going home?*, points out, "While culture shock is caused by loss of the familiar, re-entry shock is when we have changed and the familiar no longer works for us. Successful overseas adjustments become repatriation challenges." But that is another book! I recommend *Homeward Bound* by Robin Pascoe if you want to prepare yourself.

When you Emerge from the Tunnel

The long winter of your first year is over, the sun is shining, there's a hint of promise in the air, the phone is ringing and there are entries on the calendar. You've accepted your location and you've somehow found yourself on the school's Parents' Committee and in the cross stitching circle. It doesn't matter that you can't sew, you're involved. Remember what it was like and give those following you in the tunnel a helping hand and a gentle tug. Say hello, ask a new woman for coffee, invite her children to play. Yours might be the only friendly face she's seen that day, that week, and your encouraging words can make all the difference. I so remember the many small acts of kindness (life-changingly great to me) from kind women who are up for canonisation in my eyes. The life of multi-movers is a constant rolling cycle. Take what you know and pass it on.

Linda Would Like to Recommend the Following Publications:

Homeward Bound
Robin Pascoe
Expatriate Press

A Moveable Marriage
Robin Pascoe
Expatriate Press

A Broad Abroad
Robin Pascoe
Expatriate Press

The Expert Expat
Patricia Linderman and Melissa Hess
Nicholas Brealey

Moving and Living Abroad
Albright, Cho and Austin
Hippocrene Books

Especial thanks to Katherine Prendergast and Carlanne Herzog.

When not helping others make an impact with their written words through her proofreading and editing work, Linda is working on a novel and family history.

www.goodenglishcompany.com

How to Be Happy – Naturally
Karen Bird

Karen's career in England had been very important to her. Then she moved to the Sultanate of Oman and spent ten years on a voyage of self-discovery and creativity.

Many things have made my life happy — family and friends, work, home, hobbies and holidays, being alone, a good film, a good meal, a wedding, and a birth. But until I came to Oman I didn't realise how much I relied on things outside me to feel good. What I wanted was to feel good in myself all the time, or as much as I could. And not just when I was doing special things but when I was quiet, when cooking, walking or sitting alone, I wanted everyday things to feel special too. It seemed the only way to make sense of a world which seemed crazy at times.

In England I was part of a close family and had long-lasting friends. I had enjoyed working in the mental health field for many years, in a variety of areas ranging from children in community homes to elderly people in psychiatric hospitals. I spent some years doing therapeutic group work with young people and then moved to individual support work and counselling with adults. Work was vitally important to me and my identity.

I grew up in London and loved city life, though I needed the space and fresh air of the countryside too. With plenty of physical and mental energy, I had lots of hobbies and interests in a variety of crafts. I sewed, embroidered, knitted, did pottery, photography, and dabbled with the piano and guitar. I exercised with yoga, swimming and walking, as well as occasional karate and horse riding from time to time. I wasn't the most relaxed person — I had to work at it. There were some emotional ups and downs in my private life. I had a restless streak, I was curious, searching. I loved learning new things. I had not found life easy but on the other hand I was never bored. Life could be scary and depressing but overall I found it interesting, sometimes exciting and, on rare occasions, pure bliss.

By my mid 30s I was living alone for the first time after the breakup of my first marriage. I enjoyed the freedom of coming and going as I wished, not having to discuss what to eat or what colour to paint the walls; I loved having less of a routine. I had a dog and a cat and spent a lot of time walking in Yorkshire where I then lived. I wasn't looking for another husband, not consciously that is, but I found one through a very chance meeting. Denis was working overseas and after two years of letter writing, extortionate phone bills and several visits to the Middle East where he was living, we married and I moved to Oman to be with him. Like many a self-deluded expatriate wife (I've met loads), I told myself it would be for a year or two. I saw it as a sabbatical or time out, an opportunity to review and refresh, before going back to my life at home. I got it wrong. For a start, nearly ten years on, I'm still here.

Going Down

I left England thinking I was adaptable, flexible and strong. I had always loved travel and new places. I came in a spirit of adventure and felt good but that didn't last long. My enthusiasm for this new life went out of the window fast. I missed the obvious things like family and friends. I missed my house and my things. I missed the stimulation and structure of work, colleagues, common interests, feeling useful, as though in some small way I was contributing to a more harmonious world. Work gave me space to air views and to discuss life; I was used to having a voice. I missed crowded streets, city parks, cinemas, concerts and galleries; the smell of earth, country walks, deep-rooted trees. I also missed bookshops and cafes — my two favourite haunts. I often felt tired and sometimes quite scared, and alternated between tears and rage. It felt quite unreal, like I'd walked on to a film set — and the wrong one at that. In short, I felt grief. Grief usually describes the feelings of loss after a death and, while I didn't compare my own losses to that, I believe what I felt was similar. I could identify some of the stages of shock, denial, anger and pain, then withdrawal and finally acceptance and peace that experts often describe in their studies of loss and death.

I didn't have children, not something I noticed, so to speak, in England. I had been engrossed in a career and there had never been a 'right time'. I had nephews and nieces, godchildren I was close to, as well as friends without children. I had not felt I'd missed out. But Muscat seemed to be full of young children and I felt I neither fitted in with the younger couples who planned or had a family, nor with women a bit older than me whose children had grown up. With two recently acquired teenage stepdaughters who were at school in England and only spent holidays with us, I had no sense of a peer group. I felt lonely for the first time in my life — and guilty too. It was peaceful, safe and sunny in Oman. What more could I want? With material needs taken care of, life here offered great opportunity to seek higher things but that was a frightening experience for me then.

Help!

It was a gradual process, one step forward, two steps back. The smallest things could make or break a day — a few friendly words from someone in the supermarket, walking through the old alleys selling spices in Mutrah Souq on the plus side; while my hair going wrong or having to make polite conversation at a dinner party with a dozen people I didn't know could bring on panic and tears.

It was a love-hate thing. I didn't like where we lived. For a start the villa was single storey and I felt oppressed living on the ground floor. I had spent many years in converted loft rooms. I felt I could breathe when I lived up high. Now I was living in a suburban area with neat little streets set round a complex of shops. I'd imagined something far more exotic with my senses being overpowered by new sights, sounds, smells and tastes. I did love the light though and the winter sun; months of warm evenings outside; weekends spent camping in the desert or on near empty beaches. It never was all bad, though there were days when it felt like it was.

I felt lost. I didn't recognise myself or my life. I was frustrated at having to acknowledge what I saw as my shortcomings at not fitting in, I was lonely for the first time in my life, and furious with my husband, Oman, and myself. I felt I was waiting for something else, waiting to leave, to resume my career, to live somewhere that felt more me, for life to look up.

A typical day for me was to wake tired with a heavy feeling in my chest. I'd give myself a little pep talk to get out of bed. It seemed for years I had to pull myself up by my bootstrings. At the same time I felt no one noticed, and while on the one hand I was pleased about that, I felt quite unreal for a couple of years with the effort of being cheerful and all right. It wasn't that the people were unfriendly, more that most seemed to have their lives all set up.

It sounds churlish, but for a good two years I felt this was the last place on earth I would have chosen to be. (Never mind that I DID choose it — I'd changed my mind.) The imposing barren mountains seemed inaccessible, not easy to climb or to walk. They felt like the wall of a prison with the sea hemming me in on the other side. Many times I wanted to scream. I longed for the crowds of Bombay, the traffic of Bangkok, the struggle of life in Siberia — anything that was the antithesis of Oman.

Now while I have found a way of being here that is happy and satisfying, and I believe that the place of truth is within, I still hold that there is something in the geography with which we are, as individuals, more naturally in tune. Having read books on Feng Shui, the ancient Chinese art of understanding how landscapes, buildings, room arrangements can affect your life and health, I also accept there are still places where I feel more at home. It's a personal thing — I also know many people who are happy here and don't want to leave.

Eventually, I realised that nothing happens until you take the first step, 'Grasp the nettle' as my father used to say (and he made us do it as kids just to prove that something you thought would hurt didn't when you took a firm grip). There has been a constant confirmation of 'something always turns up'. I would add, 'When you're ready, when you say yes to whatever is around'. Around this time I used a selection of Bach Flower Remedies (see later) as a positive step towards inner happiness.

Once I began to accept that this was home, that today was everything, that if it wasn't okay here, how could it be okay anywhere else, then things started to shift. My resistance had not helped: it had blocked me, kept me where I was. I have for years felt that it was the wanting something to be different that caused the hurt, and I became sure of this through my own experience. And in the many self-help books I have read, the message has always been clear — that it is not circumstances nor situations that make you unhappy, but what is inside you and how you deal with it. Who's to say that if you are unhappy in Warsaw you might not also be unhappy in Wisconsin or Wimbledon? It is easy to blame other people and exterior forces for the way you feel. But from the day I decided to call Muscat home and stop fighting, I was on the up.

I have had to think long and hard about what I truly want from life, from myself and from my relationships. I have explored uncharted, and often painful, territory as I have looked inside myself. I haven't always liked what I found, but the most important thing has been to discover the power of my own mind.

While the journey up my spiritual mountain has been far from smooth, the view from the top is breathtaking. What follows are my personal experiences on what has worked for me. Use them as a starting point for your own journey in pursuit of inner peace and natural happiness. Our tastes may be different. Keep an open mind, read, research, talk to people, explore, experiment, and expand.

Watch out for the signposts that are sure to appear. You too can find your own plateau of peace.

Go for It

Many things have helped me but some especially stand out. There have been clear turning points. It's been a challenge. I have taken jobs I would never have tried, such as teaching English and publishing. I have taken the opportunity to make friends with people I would not otherwise have met and now have friends from Iran, Poland, Holland, New Zealand, America, India, and Ireland. I have discovered new interests such as singing and snorkelling, ice skating, sculpting, and more recently playing the drums. Being here has stretched my imagination in the absence of the familiar and accepted diversions such as entertainment and educational or special interest courses I could have taken in England. I often found unexpected support in new friends, and an inner discipline to explore and help myself that I didn't know I had.

I have used many natural therapies and self-help techniques. New paths have constantly emerged and there has been much to guide and uplift me. I now have good friends in like-minded people, some of whom I met through a wonderfully creative group of people who meet regularly to discuss alternative therapies, food and diet and self-help techniques. As well as that, I have read many books on self-discovery and I've written enough journals to make several books.

Home and Away

Going home twice a year has been essential for me to keep my life going there. Family relationships and close friendships, rather than diminishing, have grown as we make the most of the time we have together. I've always made the time to be with friends when I've gone home. I haven't rushed from pillar to post, but have usually preferred to spend two or three days with fewer people. Letting go of some friends can be painful and upsetting, but travelling miles for brief conversations is tiring and unsatisfying all round. Being 4000 miles away concentrates the mind and it has certainly been easier to appreciate what is most precious in life.

After many painful leavings when I'd cry as the plane took off, I said 'enough', I had it with sadness — I wanted to feel good. One day I decided to start looking forward to coming back here. In the days leading up to departure I would consciously take off my rose-coloured spectacles and count my blessings instead, I would concentrate hard on the clear skies and azure seas, majestic sand dunes and vast red deserts, my husband Denis playing his saxophone and old tribal rugs on the marble floors. Now I no longer feel that separation, and, instead, feel both connected and released.

I have also used home leaves to catch up on those courses and have studied writing, editing, photography, massage, Reiki (a natural healing technique) and more. This has helped provide stimulation and increased skills as well as giving me the chance to meet people of like mind.

Working It Out

When I arrived in Muscat, newly married and with a suitcase full of false perceptions, not least about my own needs, the most natural first thing to do was to find work. I started out volunteering once a week at the thrift shop in the local church which gave me a small amount of structure, something to do and a way of meeting people. A four week intensive TEFL course (Teaching English as a Foreign Language) turned out to serve me well for three years. I started out teaching English to children, then to the South American wives of Denis' colleagues, which helped us all to fit in. I went on to work in one of the local adult schools and enjoyed meeting Omani people who were warm and friendly as well as generally eager to learn.

I always liked writing and had spent many hours writing letters home about my life here. As a child I would tell my sister and brother stories in bed, and wrote the beginnings of stories as well as poetry and prose. Writing seemed one of the few things that really made sense to do by correspondence, and in a burst of inspiration and energy I went into The London School of Journalism and signed up for a freelance journalism course. Through it I gained the confidence to contact editors in Muscat and Dubai about freelance work. Only a year later I was offered a job in a local publishing company.

For two and a half years I earned money from writing, researching news stories and articles. I learned to proof read, and took photographs too. I was enjoying opportunities I had only previously dreamed of. I met the Russian State Ballet and local artists and went to Sri Lanka and Jordan to do travel features. I reviewed hotels and restaurants and met people who have become good friends. I learned a lot, not least about myself. It was an exercise in transferring skills. I could use my people skills and was good at PR. But I was still new to much of it, and gradually younger and more experienced people came in.

With little chance to develop myself further it became time to move on but I panicked at the thought of not having a job. I thought I'd procrastinate without the routine and social side of work, and I'd have no income of my own, maybe I was more than a little scared of being alone with my thoughts? After much soul searching, though, I took a chance and resigned; having never allowed myself to be idle before, I felt guilty and in limbo again. But then a strange thing happened. Call it fate if you like, or 'synchronicity'. Within a few months I was offered a part time job in a second hand bookshop. I was also asked to do various writing and editing jobs. Over the next three years I worked freelance on a gardening book, company and hotel newsletters, and a travel guide on Oman. Despite my resolve I was still working.

Hands On

I started out seeing creativity in a narrow way. I thought it was just about painting pictures or writing books. I also thought that I truly wanted to be a writer. After my voyage of self-discovery I ended up with a far broader feeling of what creativity was about and a craving to use my hands. About this time, I dragged myself to an exhibition to support a friend and in the true synchronistic fashion, I was introduced to a woman called Sally Ricketts who had not long arrived. Sally was a sculptor with both kiln and day. She didn't give lessons but liked people working alongside her at her home.

Sally uses a variety of clays to make full size portrait heads. With a fascination for the traditional costume of Oman, she has incorporated the colourful and ornate dress into figures of women and children, and men as well. Her abundantly green garden, where we work in the winter months, also contains bird houses and huge planters in the shape of strange faces on the house walls. My time with Sally has been wonderful. Small groups of people meet there every day of the week. Sally provides a great ambience and opportunity to explore yourself freely without any demands. We use no wheels, only hands. I have taken up sculpting which I discovered I love, and my husband's head now sits in our hallway along with small abstract figures, candle holders and burners for essential oils as well as vases and bowls.

Yet while I pondered about my long term ambitions I kept returning to the idea that aromatherapy massage could well be an ideal career option. I had used essential oils for 12 years or so, in the bath and in burners around the house. I'd had massages and had found it relaxing and stabilising in times of stress. I loved the smells of the oils and, with increasingly good immunity, I realised their therapeutic value too. It was at this time that I met astrologer Maggy van Krimpen at the Writers' Circle. She specialised in guidance on careers. At my reading she told me to use my hands. This gave me faith in my own inclinations and I went on to enrol with an aromatherapy school in London that ran a course for students overseas.

Then I heard of the ancient healing technique of Reiki (see later) through Valerie Lee, the reflexologist I was going to. She'd just done a course with a visiting Reiki Master/Teacher who was planning a return visit. I didn't understand much about it and was mildly curious. But just before the teacher arrived I suddenly felt a strong interest and a clear certainty that it was for me. After the first course I had a very happy year indeed. This led me to be certain that I should take the second level when I was next in England. This time the result was completely different and very unexpected. Although at the end of the weekend course I had a sense of being in the right place in myself, six weeks later back in Oman, I became very tired. Low moods alternated with anger in the following few months, and things I felt I had long sorted out raised their heads. It seemed everything in my life was up for review: friends, marriage, home, work, my behaviour; my whole lifestyle in fact. Situations became frustrating, things stopped working as smoothly as they had, and I noticed people often cancelled arrangements with me at the last minute, I carried on working at the two jobs I had editing a newsletter and working in the secondhand bookshop. At first, I was convinced my changing hormones were causing this havoc, but my friend in England who did the course with me was also feeling unsettled. We discovered that we felt similar with stages of ill health, tiredness; we were upset and angry, not wanting to do the things we usually did, with a sense of going into retreat. I was even more convinced that when things outside appear not to be working then there's only one place to go — within. The effect of the Reiki was that I at last began to surrender to my instinct and relax. A calm was descending. I believed I was taking it easy at last but — I was still working.

On the Up

Then, a year ago, nine years into my decade in Muscat, we moved house. I had wanted to move for a while to something that felt more like mine. It was time. In an idle moment, daydreaming, I wrote down all I wanted — a private room in which to work, balconies with a sea view, a patio garden with bushes and trees and wooden units in a kitchen large enough to have a table at which we could eat. I wanted to walk to restaurants, the shops, and the sea. I put the list away out of sight and, unusually for me, out of mind. We gave notice to our landlord, yet had nowhere to go.

I occasionally drove around the area I liked but saw nothing to rent. A few weeks before we were due to move out I drove past the road where we now live and felt a definite pull in my chest. An inner voice told me that my house was there and to be patient. A few days later I looked in the paper, saw a house to rent (there had been very few) and viewed it the next day. It was my house in every detail. It was in exactly the road where I felt it would be. In ten days we had the keys and we moved in after three weeks. I attribute this bit of magic to a combination of the law of attraction at work, being absolutely clear of what I wanted while at the same time letting it go. I knew that if I had tried to force the hand of fate it could block the natural chain of events.

With the keys in early May and the house still being repainted, we took fold-up chairs, sundowners and snacks and spent a week of evenings on the roof of the empty house, looking out to the sea. We could smell the perfume of unidentified flowers, and flocks of parrots flew over our heads as the sun set in the trees. With a small shopping centre just across the road, some restaurants, and a large car park next to the beach, it may not sound so alluring to everyone, but to me, the sound of cars and seeing people walking around, were just bliss. And it so happened that for our first two evenings on the roof there were dramatic lightening storms, but no rain, which we sat watching for hours, entranced. We both love storms, a rare occurrence here, and we took it as a welcome and felt very glad.

The day we moved in was when my shoulder seized up. I couldn't sleep that first night for the pain. I wandered around the house and at 5 am in the kitchen. And it was there that I noticed a kind of gentle breath move through the ground floor like a wave. My husband said the next day it was a sigh of relief.

But the pain in my shoulder did not go away and I still felt tired. I began meditating daily with a tape by a Buddhist called Maitreya, who has a Japanese garden and meditation centre near where I live in England. His voice is comforting and powerful. The feeling of wanting to retreat was important and I could have taken more notice than I did. In fact, I am sure it's because I ignored that feeling earlier that my shoulder seized up to tell me to stop. Even then I couldn't and kept on working though I could neither drive nor write. But eventually I got the message and when I finally stopped working altogether the pain and tiredness eased. This, for me, was the final and vital step. I let go at last.

Now that I lived by the beach, I used it — never mind that it was 100° F outside. For the first time I did not mind the heat and walked every day which seemed to help. I felt more peaceful — if sweaty — and in the right place. I began using Reiki again too and by the time I went home in August I felt much more healthy and relaxed.

Eight weeks in England restored me as always. I spent time with family and friends and got a good dose of London air. I came back to Oman truly resolved not to take any work at all — a complete breakthrough for me as I'd always worked, my biggest fear being losing a professional identity. But I felt stronger, clearer in my mind than I'd been for a long time, with different ideas forming about what was important in life. Peace of mind was becoming a priority, which meant understanding and letting go of the thoughts that prevented this. A line from Marianne Williamson's book *A Return to Love Or a Course in Miracles* comes to mind: "Do you prefer to be right or happy?"

Going On

I am much more relaxed now and I know how to take the best care of myself. I know what I want, when I want it — I listen to and trust myself. I am beginning to realise the power of my mind and the unlimited creative potential we all have. I enjoy my own company and spend more time alone, while friendships are closer and my marriage is good. Doing the last level of Reiki training in April 1998 has brought a feeling of a circle joined and a greater peace. Opportunities to do things I like keep turning up.

I'm getting better at noticing what I call 'first thoughts', the gut ones that often get silenced by our old friend the censor. Practising acting on them though is a great lesson in self trust, and I waste less energy wondering, storing things up. At last, I procrastinate less. My closest friends feel the change. Margaret said, I looked different and very happy and Ewa said "You have stopped!" Denis finds me lovely to live with and allows me to be who I am.

As I sit here on my balcony listening to the lilting call to prayer and with the smell of Jasmine and Frangipani hanging thickly on the evening air, I feel at peace. I no longer feel like I'm in a waiting room — a journey yes, never ending, ongoing, and I am open to whatever comes next. I can see more clearly and at the same time nothing matters but the present. I have no work and less interest in that than ever before. I have stopped longing for things I don't have and no longer feel the loss of the longing. I am not constantly planning for the future. I feel at this moment in connection with my true inner self and the source of all life. Things are going well. There's an ease. I am learning how to be. And being is happy — naturally.

Karen Would Like to Share Details of the Following Natural Therapies With You:

Aromatherapy and Massage

Aromatherapy is a holistic therapy that takes account of the whole person and his or her lifestyle. It uses essential oils distilled from plants to treat a whole range of physical and emotional problems as diverse as, for example, tiredness and stress, stiff muscles, cystitis and high blood pressure. A qualified therapist will make up your individual blend based on assessment of your physical and emotional state at the time. The oils must be diluted in a vegetable carrier oil, and are most powerfully used in massage to combine a hands-on, treatment that leaves most people feeling, at the very least, wonderfully relaxed. It is also a fast and enjoyable way of getting the therapeutic properties of the oils into the body. Regular massage with essential oils stimulates the body's own defence mechanisms and brings about balance, so it is a good preventative technique. With or without using oils, massage has a powerful effect on general health, by improving circulation and digestion, and stimulating the lymphatic system. It helps release emotional as well as muscular tension, and is a great way to feel comforted and looked after. Massage brings relaxation and balance at all levels – body, mind and spirit too.

Massage has helped me in stressful times at work, with backache, tiredness and during the months when my first marriage broke up, it helped keep me sane.

The benefits of massage are cumulative. When I was doing the intensive practical part of my aromatherapy course, we all gave and received a full body massage every day for eight days. By day seven I felt I was about to levitate off the couch under the hands of my Latvian co-student, and took hold of the sides just in case. By the end of the course I felt so open and filled with a sense of well-being, that as I made my way across London back to my parents, I found myself touching complete strangers in the street who asked me for directions. I must have looked like a walking A–Z, so many people approached me.

Reflexology

The origins of reflexology go back thousands of years. It is both a diagnostic tool and a treatment in itself. Like acupuncture and shiatsu, reflexology works with the lines of meridian energy flowing through the body, on which traditional Chinese medicine is based. The therapist presses on specific points, usually with the thumbs, which link with a network of nerves connected to all the organs and muscles of the body. Through this she can identify areas of tension, blocks in energy and specific problems. This treatment helps clear away blocks, encourages circulation, and generally helps restore balance, vitality and therefore, health to the body. Reflexology feels wonderful. At the very least, like massage, it is relaxing. After my first session I could hardly stand up. I made the mistake of stopping off at the supermarket and when I tried to speak to someone I knew my speech was so slurred she must have thought I was drunk. I felt wonderful the next day, however, I found reflexology very comforting as a treatment but much of that was as much to do with the therapist, Valerie Lee. She provided a secure ambience, with soft lighting, relaxing music and candles, as well as a most comfortable chair. She was very peaceful to be with and after the initial consultation, she worked quietly, often with her eyes closed, but gave me her full attention when I talked and in the first few sessions I found myself offloading a lot of what was on my mind. It was a great release emotionally and helped me relax and feel cared for.

Bach Flower Remedies

These simple flower essences are a great way of helping yourself. In my first few years here I relied on Bach Remedies a lot, discovered by a doctor and biologist Edward Bach in the 1930s, the remedies are based on his belief that happiness is a natural state of being, and that unhappiness is the cause of ill-health. The 38 remedies treat states of mind rather than symptoms and like other natural therapies they stimulate and balance the body's own resources. They are safe and simple to use, fine for children, animals and even for plants. There are people qualified to advise you on which to choose and you can visit the Dr Bach Centre at the cottage where he lived in England for a consultation. When I visited some years ago, I sat quietly in Dr Bach's peaceful room on the same wood chairs he made for himself, overlooking the garden, where the remedies are still produced in the same way.

My experience of Bach remedies is that they deal with things in layers, as and when you are ready to do so. I'd take remedies like Walnut for protection in times of change, Scleranthus for indecision, White Chestnut for unwanted thoughts, two drops in water or four under the tongue — for a couple of weeks. Then I'd forget to take them, which was a sign to me that I no longer needed them. The change would be subtle, I'd suddenly realise I felt better. Maybe weeks or months later another part of me would present itself. These days I don't think to take them but I always keep a bottle of Rescue Remedy in the house, a combination of five remedies for shock or short term stress.

Astrology

I enjoyed the only astrological reading I've ever had. I had mixed feelings about the whole subject, what with horoscopes in the dailies, I felt sure we must be influenced by the universe out there. When I was thinking about ways of working in the future, I met Maggy van Krimpen, an astrologer with a special interest in career guidance. I gave her my details over the phone — date, time and place of birth — and a few weeks later I went to her house where she interpreted my chart. Analysing the three main areas of planetary arrangement at the time of my birth, Maggy talked about the various aspects of my personality and how conflicts can arise when these are not fully understood.

Maggy talked as though she was an old friend who knew me very well, which of course she didn't before working on my chart. She helped clarify some contradictions and the potential difficulties these can cause, as well as giving me guidance on how to enhance innate abilities and skills. She highlighted some specific events in my life, and got close to their dates, which I found disconcerting, as though I could not have avoided some things that had happened to me, but she explained it was just that I was vulnerable to that kind of thing.

She spoke of how important it has been for me to use my intellect, which I agreed with — but that stronger in my chart was, a more primitive person who must use her hands. She suggested aromatherapy to start with, which I'd been considering, but said I'd go on to do other things with my hands, and I have that with Reiki, sculpting, bio-energy — and when I do these things I feel in tune with myself. Listening again to the tape of my reading in order to write this, I am reminded of Maggy saying that I have a lot of physical energy that I often don't make the most of and how I need to make more of a noise. In the past year I have been craving being able to dance — which I do in privacy at home and more recently drumming has helped me feel more balanced and on track.

Counselling and Psychotherapy

Some brief psychotherapy in London helped clear my mind a couple of years after I came to Oman. I was feeling bogged down, couldn't think straight and knew I needed someone outside of this situation to help me make sense of it. The therapist at the Group Analytic Practice was not your blank screen, Freudian type, but challenged the way I was thinking and offered practical suggestions as to how I could look at my situation differently and take more responsibility for myself. For example, she directed me to an organisation called International Social Services and although I got nowhere with that, it was good to meet with people in London and start thinking about other things I could do. Three sessions of counselling with a psychologist here two years ago, similarly helped when I wanted to talk over some of the changes I was going through with an objective professional. Friends are good to talk to and I have always done that too, but there are times when you need someone uninvolved with you who can see things in a fresh and clear way, who will challenge what you say and not let you kid yourself — not always easy for friends.

Meditation and Visualization

There are many ways to meditate in order to quiet the mind. You need to get closer to your real self, to reach a different place of consciousness and a happier state of being. During meditation the brain slows down to alpha waves, and the heart and metabolism slow down as well, which produces a relaxed but alert state. Methods include breath counting or repeating a mantra, focussing on a flower or candle flame. Having used various techniques over the last 25 years, and not had much success with the sitting cross-legged, counting breaths kind, I prefer more active visualizations where you imagine or see things in your mind to work on. I have used visualisation — or imagework as Dina Glouberman calls it in her excellent book *Life Choices and Life Changes Through Imagework* — for guidance on how to do something such as write this, for improving my health or relationships, for understanding what I really want, for solving problems, for renewing energy and more.

As well as all this, I often feel in a meditative state when I do pottery and sculpting, when I walk alone on the beach, when I dance or sing, when I daydream, and sometimes when I drum. Meditation for me is anything that brings us into the moment, to a quieter place deep inside, when the everyday world with its worries goes away and there's contentment instead.

Osteopathy

I gradually became more interested in the mind-body link. The more I read and took note of my physical feelings and discomforts, the more they made sense as messages and opportunities to change something instead. A long-term back problem recurred when I first came to Oman; I assumed it was stress. It came on after flying, sitting at the computer for a long time or after I'd been upset. With more time and opportunity to explore other avenues, I went to Katia Twyford, an osteopath here who applied a cranial-sacral technique.

As well as working on my physical body using various movements, less dramatic and more gentle than osteopathy often is — she seemed able to tune into more subtle energies and used visualisation and symbols to help me get in touch with emotional issues which were creating physical blocks. During treatment the therapist feels the pulse of cerebrospinal fluid in the brain and spine, which gives information about the body, and is effective with many bodily conditions.

I became conscious in the first couple of sessions that my head had never felt comfortable on my neck, as though it was too heavy and not straight. After six sessions over some months I was surprised to find my head and neck feeling aligned. I remember walking along the beach after my last session feeling strong, straight and light. It felt great. Now my back gives me few problems, and when it occasionally does I say thank you for the reminder that I need to stop.

Reiki

It is thought that *Reiki* originated in Tibet but it was rediscovered by Dr Mikao Usui in the mid 1800s, and brought to Japan. This ancient healing technique uses natural energy to balance the whole being by placing the hands on various points of the body. It works at all levels — physical, mental, emotional and spiritual — to bring harmony and health. *Reiki* also seems to be a catalyst for increasing awareness of the spiritual self and brings about inevitable change. The *Reiki* philosophy is simply to not anger or worry just for today, to honour parents, teachers and elders, to earn your living honestly, to bless what you have and be kind to every living thing.

Each level of training takes two to four days of theory and practice, with what are known as attunements, a ritual specific to *Reiki* training, to open or attune you to the energy of *Reiki*. There are no tests or exams, and it is up to each person to use *Reiki* after the attunements, to develop it for themselves. First degree *Reiki* is primarily for self-healing, while the second degree of *Reiki* enables you to send the energy over time and space for distance healing and the third and last level is that of Reiki master and teacher.

Both giving and receiving *Reiki* is a relaxing and enjoyable experience. The person receiving lies on a couch fully clothed, while the person or persons giving it place their hands on various positions on the body for a few minutes in each place. It can be comforting and relaxing both to give and receive. Gentle music often plays in the background and usually the session is carried out quietly. The hands of the giver often become warm, which the receiver can usually feel, and hands may tingle, especially around problem areas.

Bio-energy

A visiting therapist from Ireland, Patricia Rafferty, introduced bio-energy to the UK a few years ago. Bio-energy is a great mix of science and mysticism, as well as a powerful healing tool that has had some amazing results. Patricia uses this practical healing technique to work on the energy field or aura surrounding the body. The theory behind bio-energy is that past trauma, accidents, surgery or distress, whether physical or emotional, are held in the energy field. Healing can happen spontaneously as the person takes care of his or herself, but often it seems that a painful memory remains until it is released and healed by someone like Patricia who has the ability, sensitivity and skill to feel, and often see, the human energy field.

I had a course of treatment myself when Patricia first came, more out of curiosity than anything else. She picked up an old upset which she worked on in four sessions of half an hour on consecutive days. These induced a feeling of comfort and safety after which I felt happier and physically and emotionally more at ease. Patricia works close to the body, using her hands to feel out any irregularities in the energy field, and swirling them around in circles as she removes any blocks. Sometimes I felt warm, sometimes cold, and my body swayed back and forth at times. Then she places her hands on points of the body such as shoulder and hip to bring further balance.

Music

Music has always played a large part in my life and I have appreciated that even more here. I have sung in a choir and have entertained friends who play various instruments and sing. I now take drum lessons, though I have no aspirations to be in a rock band. As well as being a great stress reliever, drumming gives me a satisfaction that is hard to describe. I am hooked — the more I do the more I want to do. I read an article recently about how drumming synchronises the left and right hemispheres of the brain, and another on how in America, Mickey Hart of Grateful Dead fame, has been working with the healing and therapeutic effects of playing drums.

Writing with a Difference

Wanting to explore writing further I went on a workshop called *Write to Life* in London in 1994, run by Nigel Watts, an author of four books. The course encouraged us to put the editor or inner critic aside, initially by giving it a name and a form and banishing it to the other side of the room. We did group exercises to encourage communication and trust, meditated, walked, wrote short timed pieces and read them out without comment from others.

This workshop brought together a diverse group of men and women aged from 20s — 50s, from a lawyer to a trapeze artist, as well as several aspiring and published writers. By the close of the weekend we inevitably felt close. I still meet up with the woman I paired up with for the last exercise.

Write to Life was based on the work of an American writer and teacher, Natalie Goldberg, who applies her Zen and Buddhist principles to writing. Back in Muscat and with a new enthusiasm, I joined the Writers Circle and suddenly found an outlet for self expression that gave me confidence and strength. The other members were a mixture of people who just liked to write as well as those who had had short stories, poems and articles published. Putting my inner critic aside, I began to enjoy reading out what I'd written and having a voice. I was less interested in being published than in the feeling of trust in the group and in awe at the creativity that poured forth, I wrote most days and began to feel freer than I had done for a while as I explored myself and experimented with a new me through the words.

Then my yoga teacher and friend, a New Zealander called Andrea, showed me a book she thought I'd be interested in — *The Artist's Way*, by Julia Cameron. This book is set out as a twelve week self-study course in discovering and recovering creativity, as Cameron puts it, with a spiritual bent; it's a course in self-nurturing and self-trust. Exercises asked me to remember childhood things I'd liked, to explore imaginary lives, to look at who and what supported me best, and I found I rather liked being my own counsellor. Once I'd started I could not put the book down. I worked on it religiously every week — the reading, the exercises and the mainstay of the course — what Cameron calls *morning pages*.

Morning pages are three pages of writing without stopping, without thinking. You just keep the pen moving and write out all immediate junk in your mind. Writing quickly gives the inner critic, your own censor, less time to get a hold. It helps you move away from left brain activity of logic and intellect, away from ego thinking, and gets you more into creative right brain stuff — and hence closer to your less conscious self, a self that seems wiser, more interesting, nearer the spirit of your truer self.

I loved *morning pages*. I wrote them with great ease and still do, though their content has changed. In the early days my notebooks were full of negatives, moans and complaints about how I felt, people, lack of things missed. I also found myself writing about painful events from my distant past that I had never explored. That was not so easy. For days, maybe weeks, I'd have the feeling someone was looking over my shoulder but I braved it, got past the fear of putting things into words and breathed a sigh of relief.

Over the next three months I realised there was a change. I complained less, I saw my surroundings more positively; I'd be driving along, for example, and I'd suddenly look at the trees lining the highway or the light on the mountains and feel thankful. After about three pages it was as if my subconscious took over and the magic began. Snippets of stories, paragraphs, people with names I didn't know would unexpectedly appear on the page, written by me but not consciously. These days my pages contain almost no negatives, but explore ideas, ways of being, new thoughts. After a few pages my writing can change, it slows down and becomes smaller. I feel relaxed and words come but I don't know what they will be. Sometimes a kind of poetry appears, to inspire me, encourage me, clear messages of how to be.

The Artist's Way is about creativity in the widest, wildest sense. It is about finding your authentic self and being true to that whether it's working at what you enjoy, cooking a meal, cleaning the house, painting a picture or growing plants. Cameron urges kindness in doing so. Through this course I became more aware of what makes me tick and became a best friend to myself.

Cameron talks too about synchronicity — Carl Jung's term for a seemingly positive order in events, Cameron says when we get what we ask for it's easier to call it coincidence or luck, rather than admit maybe something intelligent and responsive is at work in the universe. But it is true that once you make a commitment, no matter how small, wonderful things start to happen that seem a lot more than luck.

Books and CDs

Creative Visualization
Shakti Gawain
Bantam New Age

Life Choices and Life Changes through Imagework
Dina Glouberman
Mandate

Wild Mind
Natalie Goldberg
Rider

The Artist's Way
Julia Cameron
Pan Macmillan

A Course in Miracles Foundation for Inner Peace
Penguin
Anatomy of the Spirit
Caroline Myss
Bantam

Aromatherapy – For Healing the Spirit
Gabriel Mojay
Gaia

The Everyday Meditator – a practical guide
Osho
Newleaf

CDs

Complete Relaxation and Meditation
Buddha Maitreya
http://www.buddhamaitreya.co.uk/shop.html

The Abraham Tapes
Abraham-Hicks Publications
http://www.abraham-hickslawofattraction.com/
lawofattractionstore/index.html

Other Useful Books

Mind to Mind
Betty Shine
Corgi

Hands of Light
Barbara Ann Brennan
Bantam New Age

Light Emerging
Barbara Ann Brennan
Bantam New Age

Writing Down the Bones
Natalie Goldberg
Shambala

Feel the Fear and Do It Anyway
Susan Jeffers
Arrow

Mind and Movement
Tony Crisp
Daniel

Passage to Power
Leslie Kenlon
Century Vermilion

Creating Sacred Space with Feng Shui
Karen Kingston
Piatkus

A Return to Love
Marianne Williamson
Thorsons

Chi Kung
James MacRitchie
Element

Shamanism – as a Spiritual Practice for Daily Life
Tom Cowan
The Crossing Press

Soul Retrieval
Sandra Ingerman
Harper Collins

Conversations with God
Neale Donald Walsch
Hodder & Stoughton
The Well of Creativity Interviews
Michael Toms
New Dimensions

Simple Abundance
Sarah Ban Breathnach
Bantam

Being Happy!
Andrew Matthews
Media Masters

There are many good books available on *Reiki*, *Aromatherapy*, *Reflexology*, and *Bach Remedies*.

Bach Flower Remedies are available in most pharmacies and health food shops.

The Dr Edward Bach Healing Centre: http://www.colourtherapyhealing.com/colour_therapy/nature/bach_flower_remedies.php

The London School of Journalism: www.lsj.org

Karen is currently enjoying exploring and reflecting on what is most essential in her life at this time and is open to new opportunities.

Resilience: Learning How to Fly Like Eagles
Sarah Koblow

*A social worker and serial expat shares
her personal story of what it means to be
resilient despite the relocations*

In Transition

Making the most of a rainy summer day, I was
teaching my sixteen-year-old daughter how to make
Boeuf Bourguignon in the country kitchen of our
Brittany stone cottage. This had been our home for
three years when we lived in France and now provided
a peaceful haven in our ever-moving life. We are a
British passport holding family in the middle of our
fifth relocation and describe ourselves as *Une Famille
Internationale* in response to the dreaded question, "so
where are you from?"

"Mum, you know when I start at The American School
in Doha?" Jenny asked as she stirred the red *Le
Creuset* pan.

"Mmm, you mean in two weeks time," I glanced up from my laptop and wondered where this conversation was going.

"Well, will it be my eighth or ninth school?" she asked. I counted all the school gates I had watched her disappear through and maternal angst flooded me.

"Actually, it'll be your tenth including the different kindergartens and the time back in England during the Gulf War!" My mouth twisted into a grimace and I felt slightly queasy.

We were officially in 'transition' — temporarily displaced with huge chunks of normal life misplaced. I knew I would find my iPhone recharger, probably in the last cardboard box I would unpack in Qatar in a month's time. Yet, I needed it now, in France, to get in touch with my WWWs (Worldwide Wonderful Women) to help me through this latest revelation and the ensuing guilt trip.

Teaching Resilience to our Third Culture Kids

As a social worker and counsellor, I am all too aware of the effects that constant change and loss could be having on my three, "Third Culture Kids." The number one bi-product of choosing to live internationally has to be the wave of emotions we all feel every time we sit our children down and tell them to say goodbye to their friends and, "Don't worry, you can Skype."

During my expat journey, I have been forced to fly many times by the challenges inherent in this chosen lifestyle. If I am being honest, there is another side to this expat flying game. If I am being really honest there are times when I have felt more like a Dodo than an Eagle. My usual default mode in tough times is humour — when all else fails, find something to laugh about. However, when we are done laughing in the face of adversity, how do we start dealing with loss and pain? What do we do when the pain spreads to our children?

Have you ever thought about what you would do or feel if your worst nightmare came true? Maybe like me, you have heard the word cancer spoken over you by a consultant and felt the ultimate betrayal of your own body turning against you and threatening your life.

How would you respond to questions such as, "Mummy are you going to die?" This scene would have been no less painful had it happened to us back 'home' in England. However, being an expat adds a whole other layer of adversity. Coping with cancer was difficult enough but I was also in an Arabic hospital and world. For example, this meant coming round from surgery with no pain relief, which we then had to fight for.

Stress experts agree that changes of job, school or home and loss of loved ones can be detrimental to our mental and physical health. As global nomads we have chosen a life that produces menacing levels of stress on a regular basis.

International mobility is like the government warning on a packet of cigarettes. I did not have a choice about developing thyroid cancer, but we have chosen to make our children international. Choosing this life-style could seriously damage our health. Just like passive smoking, our children will be inhaling potentially toxic emotional fumes. By its very nature 'expatland' has adversity built into its mainframe as we experience loss continually because someone is always leaving. That is why we need to be more proactive than the average world citizen in learning resilience.

The good news is that experts in positive psychology are finding that adversity can also be beneficial for us. Resilience research throughout the world, conducted in different countries and cultures, has proved the universal truth in the old adage, "what doesn't kill you makes you stronger."

Psychologists define resilience as, "The universal capacity which allows a person, group or community to prevent, minimize or overcome the damaging effects of adversity." [Grotburg, 2003 p1]

I personally prefer the Australian version. "Resilience is the happy knack of bungy jumping through the pitfalls of life." [Fuller, 1998 p2]

Resilience is not like the colour of your eyes, fixed at the point of conception. It is a skill that can be learned by anyone. It is also a muscle, which, like all muscles, gets stronger the more you use it. There is a wealth of literature about resilience readily available through Amazon, but I think in the end it boils down to one thing: choice. All of us expat Dodos can choose to grow resilient wings and learn how to use them whatever crisis we face.

A Lesson in Resilience

It was a sunny May morning in our modern rental home in The Hague. I was woken early by my husband's goodbye kiss as he left for a business meeting in London. Snuggling back under my feather duvet, I was tempted to go back to sleep but remembered that my girls were starting exams that day.

"I'll treat them to pancakes," I decided as I leapt out of bed. Jenny, fifteen, Emma, twelve and Josh nearly eleven, usually helped themselves to Weetabix on school mornings, but I wanted to spoil them. They had settled well in Holland despite a tough beginning including experiencing bullying and the restructuring of their dad's job — with the possibility of redundancy. We survived the re-shuffle but several of our new friends had already been forced to repatriate. We loved our Dutch life and very much wanted to stay.

Our black Labrador, Ren, started barking loudly downstairs so I hurried down the wooden spiral staircase to let him out into the garden. Walking into the sleek modern kitchen, I caught a glimpse of Phoebe, our golden Labrador under the table. Ren was standing near her, continually barking so I shouted in my best Mary Whitehouse voice, "Stop!"

His ears flattened and he cowered before me as I finally noticed what he was barking at. Phoebe was not in her usual, curled up position on her favourite blanket. Her legs were sticking straight out from her body and she was not breathing.

"Oh, no!" I began to cry as I fell to my knees and cuddled her. She was still warm. "What should I do? What about the kids?" My mind raced. Rushing to the door I shouted up the three-storey staircase, "Don't come into the kitchen, there's a bit of a mess," desperately trying to buy myself time to think.

Having read the *Arriving in Holland* booklet from cover to cover just months earlier, I knew that there was no advice about what to do with a beloved, very large, very dead dog in your kitchen. I was on my own with a big problem, again.

I momentarily flirted with the idea of hiding her in the adjoining garage and pretending nothing had happened. However, the memory of the pain experienced when I recently slipped a disc while vacuuming deterred me from following this Pythonesque option.

My emotionally intelligent children make it very difficult for me to pull the wool over their eyes at the best of times so I quickly opted for what has worked in the past — being open with them, then supporting them in looking at options and choices.

Going back upstairs, I called all three into my bedroom and shared the sad news, as calmly as possible. I could not help crying.

"Thank goodness," Jenny sighed deeply.

I was alarmed by her apparent callousness, which was very out of character.

"What do you mean?" I asked.

"I could hear you were upset when you shouted not to come into the kitchen," she explained, her voice hesitant with emotion, "and, and, I... I thought something had happened to Dad," she explained. "I'm upset about Phoebe, but glad it isn't Dad," she sobbed.

"Come on let's snuggle, cuddle," I comforted them all with our family invitation for a group hug in my bed. We let the tears flow, then we did the most resilient thing anyone can do when faced with painful adversity — 'phone a friend'. Number One Rule of Resiliency: you do not have to cope or suffer alone.

The power of the WWWs immediately kicked in. I phoned several, none of whom knew what to do but they checked the Worldwide Web, contacted the *Dieren* (animal) Ambulance and arranged for them to come at lunchtime.

How did we cope in the interim?

Jenny, having worked hard for important exams literally got on her bike, and on with the job in hand. A girl who had seen both granddads die suddenly and held her mum's hand through cancer treatment was able to keep her head "when all around were losing theirs." She cried later.

Josh quickly asserted, "No, I don't want to go to school today, I want to stay home and say goodbye."

Emma, who was closest of all to Phoebe, at first tried to do it her big sister's way by soldiering on. Driving her to school (as she was now very late), I could see her begin to crumble as the shock wore off and grief set in. My dilemma was whether to protect her and insist she come back home, or to let her learn to fly solo.

On hearing our latest Koblow adversity tale, her caring form tutor gently intervened, insisting Emma "was more important than the exam" which she could re-sit anytime. Emma decided to return home where, together with Josh and Ren, we covered Phoebe in tulips and made a tear-filled goodbye to our much-loved pet.

When Dad returned from London a couple of days later, we were all surprised and touched by how visibly shaken he was. A proclaimed cat lover, he had seemed to tolerate rather than embrace our canine family members. He beckoned me up to the privacy of our bedroom where he broke down and sobbed into my shoulder. Being a foot taller than me, he had to stoop.

"I've lost my job," he wept as another crisis crash landed in our family life. Redundancy threatened the home and country we lived in, the school our children went to, as well as our income.

Taking his face in my hands, it was not without wishful thinking or false hope that I assured him, "It'll be alright. We'll be okay."

Developing resilience does not mean that we will be immune to sadness and fear when adversity strikes. The Chinese word for crisis is made up of two characters, danger and opportunity. At the heart of every crisis can be awesome opportunities. This latest crisis we faced was another opportunity for my husband and me to practice flying and teach our eaglets resilience in the process. Eaglets learn to fly primarily by observing their parents; it is a learned skill not an instinct.

So, if you are feeling like an expat Dodo in your international circumstances look around you for flying eagles, and watch how they use their resilient muscles, observe the detail. Flex your wings, find some thermal uplift in resilient friends and give soaring a go.

Our fifth international move was forced on us, but has given us opportunities to fly higher than we would ever have thought we could. One month after arriving in Qatar I became a published author and poet in *Turning Points*, which became an Amazon bestseller. The whole Koblow family is soaring in the warmth of that uplift. This has been the smoothest transition yet thanks to my WWW team so easily reachable on the WWW. That is of course as soon as I unpack all those cardboard boxes and find my recharger.

My Top Five Resiliency Tips

1. Adversity is part of life. Bad things happen to good people including our children.
2. Resiliency is a life skill anyone can learn.
3. Like a muscle it increases with strength the more we use it.
4. We can teach our children this powerful bounce-back ability.
5. The best way to teach our children how to fly is to show them.

For me resiliency is the hope that we can face and find ways to move through our pain, towards overcoming our circumstances, with the right attitude and support.

Sarah Would Like to Share the Following Resources With You:

Books

Turning Points
Kate Cobb (et al including Sarah Koblow)
Summertime Publishing

The Resilience Doughnut: The Secret of Strong Kids
Lyn Worsley
Griffin Press

Emotional Resilience and The Expat Child
Julia Simens
Summertime Publishing

Third Culture Kids: Growing Up Among Worlds
David C. Pollock and Ruth E Van Reken
Nicholas Brealey Publishing
Raising Global Nomads
Robin Pascoe
Expatriate Press

*Teenagers: What every Parent has to Know and
The Sixty Minute Series*
Rob Parsons
Hodder and Stoughton

Expat Teens Talk
Dr Lisa Pittman and Diana Smit
Summertime Publishing

*Changes that Heal: How to Understand your
Past to Ensure a Healthier Future*
Dr Henry Cloud
Zondervan

*Boundaries Series including Boundaries With
Your Kids*
Dr Henry Cloud and Dr John Townsend
Zondervan

Expat Life Slice by Slice
Apple Gidley
Summertime Publishing

I am a mother, counsellor and social worker. I am also a successful STAR (spouse travelling and relocating) and have lived in England, America, Bahrain, Qatar, France and Holland. I recently became a published writer and poet in an Amazon bestselling book.

Blog: countonlysunnyhours.wordpress.com
Twitter: @sarahkoblow & @turningpoints
Facebook: www.theturningpointsbook.com

Ten Tips for a Smooth Flight
Jo Parfitt

*After 25 years on the move, living before kids,
with kids, and as an empty nester, Jo shares her
top tips for a happy, meaningful life on the move.*

Being forced to fly can bring out the best in you. The anticipation of doing something strange and new for the first time is usually far worse than taking that first step. By all means think about your move in advance, but try not to worry about it. Think positively and constructively. If you discover a problem area, try to solve it, or at least find out as much as you can. Take that first step. Be proactive. Be positive. Go for it. As Julia Cameron says in her inspiring workbook, *The Artist's Way*: "Leap and the net will appear."

Tip No 1 – Research Before You Go

Evidence suggests that going to a new posting in a positive frame of mind affects your stay considerably. If you have no idea what to expect, then, chances are, you will not be feeling very positive. You may, for example, be certain that there will be no international school for your children, no photography class for you and no chance of buying Bran Flakes, all these negative thoughts will make you dread your new assignment. But worrying won't get you anywhere and assuming the worst never helps. So try to find out before you go.

The Federation of American Women's Clubs Overseas has tens of thousands of members worldwide, who would love to help you settle in, and there are many many newcomers' clubs all over the world waiting for you. Whether you want to join a professional network, a bridge club, tennis club, toddler group or one for people from your country, you will find many are listed on www.expatwomen.com, www.newcomersclub.com and www.expatica.com and many more. Check whether your company offers a resource or library online or within its offices and if not, again, there is much to be found online. I particularly like www.realpostreports.com. *The Culture Smart!* series of books are handy guides for over a hundred countries and that give the cultural low down.

It's a good idea to talk to people who have either lived in, or know someone who has lived in, the country you are moving to. It's easy to find such people online through various forums, clubs and schools. I recommend www.expatexchange.com as a site with many useful forums and networks. Unless you happen to be the first non-local person to set foot in your new location, there is bound to be a way that you can talk to someone in the know. So, if you find out that, indeed, they do not sell Marmite in Bogota, you can be prepared and take some with you.

Remember:
The more informed you are, the more positive you will become, and the better your chance of a contented life.

Tip No 2 – Be Proactive

Proactivity is just that, doing something about it. Its opposite, 'reactivity', is moaning about it, blaming others or situations but without seeing the solutions.

When I lived in Stavanger, Norway, I often used to walk round a lake for exercise. Surrounded by beautiful and inspiring scenery, it was the perfect place to think. Sometimes I would walk with my friend, Alice Hurley, who for me has long been a positive outlook role model. It was on one of these walks on a crisp autumn day, when the silver birch trees were aflame, that she described proactivity in a way that really worked for me:

"If you don't like something you are doing you can either change it, accept it, or leave it — but don't moan about it."

One way to counteract the reactivity that we all can be prey to, is to surround yourself with proactive people. We all have problems and down times and it is easy to kid ourselves that it is comforting to sit down with a cup of coffee and a relative stranger and have a good grumble. But one gripe leads to another and before long you are even more depressed than before. When you are being reactive things do not get better.

So choose your friends from among the cheerful faces you meet along the way. It may be pouring with rain for the tenth day in a row, but, as Katherine Prendergast says so poignantly 'Proactive people take their weather with them.' Look for the person whose countenance is not as grey as the leaden sky, and introduce yourself.

Tip No 3 – Build a Support Team

As an expatriate, you are automatically away from familiar surroundings, family and friends.

A support team is made up of the people you can rely on. When you are constantly on the move you have to make friends quickly. Often it can be invaluable to have a soulmate, and you can help yourself to find one. If you are a keen writer, as I am, then join or start an informal writers' group. That way you will find yourself talking to people who think like you do and appreciate the same things. People who speak the same language can be a comfort.

Find someone you can rely on in times of need. When there is a crisis you can be sure that far more people will offer help than you expected. If you make friends with people who have children of similar ages to your own, then sleepovers can help compensate for not being able to leave children with grandparents.

Try to find the names of a reliable doctor, dentist, car mechanic or electrician early on. Otherwise, you could find yourself flat on the floor with your finger over a burst pipe, unable to waste time battling with a foreign telephone operator as you try to find an emergency plumber. Keep the list of phone numbers by the telephone and relax in the knowledge that you are prepared for a crisis.

Many online forums exist specifically for many destination cities; see who you can meet before you go.

Tip No 4 – Keep in Touch

Sometimes your support team can be made up of people who live in another country. Women like to talk. When a woman has a problem she often prefers not to bottle it up and the very act of sharing her feelings can help her feel better. To have someone who understands you well on the end of a telephone, can be a great comfort, if expensive. But you don't necessarily need a phone to keep in touch.

During the ten years I was abroad before the advent of the Internet, my mother and I wrote to each other religiously every Sunday. The letters were little more than diaries, detailing the trivial and not so trivial events of the previous week. We both derived great comfort from these over the years, and when we returned home for seven years later, my mother felt at a loss on a Sunday afternoon with no one to write to. First, we wrote on blue airmail paper, later we sent faxes. Today we use email and Skype. As the years go by and good friends become better friends, I stay connected to many people via Facebook. Somehow it feels as if we have never been apart.

When email came along the number of people I correspond with mushroomed out of all proportion. The notes I send are shorter and full of typos but the thought is there and old friends are never far from my thoughts.

Keeping in touch makes your support team, even if its members are distant, feel close at hand. When we first moved to Stavanger it was as if I took my friend Gill with me. We communicated so regularly at first that I didn't feel quite so alone in a strange place. When she went to the United Arab Emirates I was there for her, ensuring I replied to her emails straight away, giving support and soothing comments.

Keeping in touch is much more than a card at Christmas. The Internet is a godsend but it cannot replace human contact. Try not to keep all your friends in cyberspace at the detriment of making new, local friends. You will discover you get more energy from face-to-face meetings than those online.

Tip No 5 – Retain Your Identity

When I lived in Stavanger I attended a workshop called 'enriching your life', we were all asked to draw a picture of how we perceived ourselves. It was amazing how many people drew themselves with their children and families. I drew myself holding a briefcase in one hand and two children in the other.

How do you picture yourself? Many people are fulfilled being a home-maker and mother alone. Others are satisfied with a demanding career and little social life. Draw a picture of how you see yourself now and then another of how you would like to be. Have you exchanged the baby for the briefcase or a tennis racket?

It is important for you to be able to be yourself despite living in a foreign location and an international community. Try to pinpoint what elements you need to have in your life in order to function as a complete and contented person, and then make every effort to ensure that you make time for them too. Be kind to yourself and you will, in turn, be kinder to everyone around you.

Tip No 6 – Treat Yourself

I heard a story the other day about a family who went to work and live overseas with the sole objective of saving every penny they earned. They lived like paupers with hardly any furniture and without a television or stereo, had no social life and never went on holiday. They went home rich. Or did they? New experiences enrich your life in a different way from money. It seems a waste to have the opportunity of experiencing another culture at first hand and then not to take it.

Though some expatriates have financial incentives for living abroad this is the case increasingly less. If you are lucky enough to receive generous travel allowances use them. But try not to always head for home, you will find that exploring the rest of the world, or the other cities close by will enrich your life considerably. I recently met an expat who told me that during her decades abroad, Friday night has always been 'eat local' night, which has had many benefits. Not only does she feel more integrated and at home, but their weekly treat has been easy on the budget too.

Living away from your roots is not easy. You need to feel that your sacrifices are worthwhile and that there are true advantages to a nomadic lifestyle.

Visit the flower markets if you live in Holland, a beer festival if you live in Germany or go to the Rodeo if you live in Houston. These little treats soften the blow, and can lift your spirits.

For me, my annual treat has been to attend a conference or training course every year. Sometimes it has been a writing course, sometimes the Families in Global

Transition or Women's International Networking conference, but I have discovered that being with like-minded people who are like me gives me a huge boost of happiness. At these places I make new friends and learn new things, which keep me going for a whole year. If I can't get away to such an event then I would either do something locally or take a course by correspondence.

Tip No 7 – Do Something Different

Every new posting brings with it a host of opportunities. If you find yourself in Indonesia with a fleet of servants, then you have time to take that distance learning course you have been talking about. If you find yourself in a land of sand dunes why not take up sandskiing or learn to dune bash in a four-wheel-drive? If you have taken on a live-in babysitter there is no reason why you shouldn't join the local choral society or drama group. Rehearsals thrice weekly are no longer a problem.

Take advantages of the things you are able to do in the new location that you would never do at home. In Dubai, Muscat and The Hague my husband has played and continues to play rhythm and lead guitar with a series of rock bands. His group, Mother Superior and the Bad Habits seized the opportunity to back up The Manfreds when they came on tour, and earned good money entertaining everyone at the company Christmas dinner too. Back in England, he was lucky to join in a jam session at the local pub. Being a big fish in a small pond gave me the chance to write features for a local woman's magazine despite my lack of experience. In the end I had to use two pseudonyms I was so busy. Back in England the chances of my finding a slot in a woman's monthly magazine were slim, if not impossible. When we moved to the Netherlands in 2005, my husband joined another band and I found plenty of writing markets again.

Being creative is a marvellous outlet for your emotions. Expatriate communities are often packed with talented, bored women, who would rather teach sculpture or silk painting for free than sit at home unable to obtain a work permit. Take advantage of these cut price courses. Sometimes you will only have to pay for your own materials.

Living in a new and exciting culture can do wonders for your imagination. It broadens the mind and fills your vocabulary, sound and sight banks with new items that you can pull out when you are creating music, words or pictures. Try keeping a diary as well as a photograph album and videos, so that you can store your rich variety experiences for the future. You never know — they could earn you some money one day.

Tip No 8 – Call it Home

Remember Alice? I told you about her in the section on proactivity. Well, Alice, and her family have been on the move almost constantly. During this time they have lived in several locations in England, Scotland, America, Indonesia, Dubai and Norway. And, subsequent to a few months settling-in period, in each new place, Alice has always worked out of the home. But one thing stands out above all others that has ensured that their life is as settled as possible — wherever they are living. They try to put down roots in almost any country or city they have inhabited, and insist that home is now. They take their furniture and all their possessions on every move. It was not until the move from a large Norwegian house to Surrey was imminent that they finally said goodbye to the pool table. As Ruth van Reken, author of *Letters Never Sent* has been heard to advise on many occasions, "My father always said we had to unpack our bags and plant our trees". It is sound advice.

Hankering after a place where you used to belong does no one any good, least of all you. So make the place you live in now your home and personalise it as best you can with memorabilia from past lives, trips and people. Blend the Indian furniture with the Bedouin rugs and Turkish copper and make each place you live uniquely your own. Make huge collages of the faces and places from each assignment and take pleasure in reliving those magic moments whenever you glance at it. For if home is where the heart is then the heart should follow too.

Tip No 9 – Explore

I can remember vividly the hours it would take to pack our four-wheel-drive for weekend camping trips into the desert when we lived in Oman. After I had packed drink coolboxes and food coolboxes, found lilos and pumps, buckets, spades, cooking utensils, tents and sunshades into the boot, Ian would roll up from work, ready to jump into his shorts and leap behind the wheel. Then, arriving home in the dark on a Friday evening (for Fridays are Sundays in that part of the world), hot, tired, thirsty and encrusted with sand and sea water, we would laboriously unpack, desand and rinse everything all over again. I used to swear it took more time to pack and unpack, drive there and back and finally pitch and unpitch camp than we actually spent there relaxing. But it was always worth it. To lie back in the warm air, listening to the waves, staring up at a velvet starscape watching out for shooting stars was a rare privilege. To have stayed at home with Sky TV and a take-away could not compare.

It can be so much easier to stay at home, but never so exciting nor enriching an experience. Diaries and photograph albums, memories even, are not made in your sitting room or front garden. Get out and about, feed your soul and develop your conversation. Learn about local sights or nature and really experience a country from the inside.

Day trips can last you a lifetime.

Tip No 10 – Get Involved

Saying 'yes' is a much repeated message in this book. And getting involved is about saying 'yes'. It is about giving up your free time to volunteer for committees you care about. It is about meeting regularly with people of like mind and doing something that interests you. It could be the school parent teacher association, or the arts centre. If you are not a committee kind of person then you can still say yes to being in a squash ladder or to joining in to play pétanque in France. If you don't like committees and hate sports then you could join in a sewing bee or take cookery classes. Getting involved in something means that you meet people. People become friends. Friends become your support team and your social life. When you are involved you start to belong. Belonging is the objective of us all.

Here I go advocating that you all have to join something, when I know only too well how much I hate making that first step. Even at a newcomers coffee morning of the Petroleum Wives Club I found myself tongue-tied and terrified of having to introduce myself. But the moment I had opened my mouth and said the first word the ice was broken and in a flash someone had handed me the telephone number of a potential babysitter in my area. I was off. I duly joined the PWC, attended one more coffee morning three weeks later and never went there again. Because three weeks later one contact had led to another and I was far too busy.

My passion is writing and so everywhere I have lived I have joined or started a writers' circle. Here I can guarantee I spend time with people who share my love of words and not only are meetings inspiring, but it's here that I make my best friends.

I am also passionate about running my own business, so in most countries I have joined, started or chaired a professional women's group, joining the board almost right away. Again this has fed me with people like me, but as an entrepreneur it has also ensured I was front and centre in the eyes of potential new clients.

So, take that first step towards involvement in just one thing, and even if that group is not your ideal choice, it can be the catalyst you need and the start of belonging.

Jo Would Like to Share the Following With You:

Conferences

Families in Global Transition
www.figt.org

Women's International Networking
www.winconference.com

Writing Courses
The Watermill at Posara
www.watermill.net

The London School of Journalism
www.lsj.org

Websites

Expatica
www.expatica.com

Expat Women
www.expatwomen.com

Expat Arrivals
www.expatarrivals.com

Paguro
www.paguro.com

Real Post Reports
www.talesmag.com

Transitions Abroad

www.transitionsabroad.com

Expat Exchange

www.expatexchange.com

Federation of American Women's Clubs Overseas

www.fawco.org

Newcomers Club

www.newcomersclub.com

PART TWO

Arrivals

"My feelings go up and down like a seesaw. One moment I am feeling on top of the world: arriving in Dubai to be given VIP treatment, speeding through the city gazing at the incredible white buildings. Then the next moment I am down again: feeling so tired, not coping with the jet lag nor the obligatory late nights attending 'welcome' functions while coping with three tired, excited and demanding Children."

Gill Beckwith in the United Arab Emirates

"We watched agape as the cages of live chickens from Azerbaijan, the wicker baskets of melons from Armenia did the tour of the luggage carousel. Waiting for our own Samsonite cases we watched African students leap to retrieve their sacking and string-bound chattels."

Bobby Meyer in the Former Soviet Union

"It is six months now since we arrived, but instead of all the things I had hoped to do, I am still busy 'moving'. We seem to take one step forward and two steps back. Oliver, never the easiest child to feed, has had to give up the Bran Flakes, which were previously the mainstay of his diet. Fortunately he has been weaned onto Oat Crunchies."

Nicki Chambury arriving in Miri, Sarawak

"When I first arrived in Houston I felt like I was living in a movie. Everything about the place had been portrayed in films before: wide streets, big hoardings, drive-in cinemas. The feeling didn't wear off for two years."

Alice Hurley in the United States of America

"Arriving is a bit like running off a cliff, cartoon-style. You keep on running at speed on thin air and are fine until you look down and lose your faith. Then you fall fast and far."

Christine Yates in Germany

"I just put my head down and get into a routine as quickly as possible, accepting all invitations. I also moan at my husband a lot."

Hilary Milne in Norway after 16 years in Cairo, Russia and more

"We had a growing sense of euphoria at having arrived after all that anticipation, then a growing sensation that Madagascar is somewhat different from Hertfordshire."

Mark Eadie in Madagascar

But Not This
Christine Yates,
English in Germany

Why is it that at thirty-four
I want to scream and run amok
And be perverse and slam the door
And do those things that I ought not?
I want no duty, must or should
No really ought or said I would —
Instead I'd rather scream and swear
And shock with words I never use
Or hurl down insults and abuse
On those whose faces I must bear.

But at my age it feels not right —
To employ adolescent tools,
To rail against the wooden rules,
The moribund smiles and easy truths.
And yet?
Which other rules am I to use?

"What DO you want?" he asks with a kiss.
"I JUST DON'T KNOW," I say.
"But not this."

Writer and editor: passionate about words and expression, creative personal development, and transitions. Ten years abroad as peripatetic execuwife; now a happily unmarried smallholder and salsa dancer.

www.journeywords.co.uk
Blog: www.journeywords.co.uk/blog.php
Twitter: @journeywords

Sick in Stavanger
Linda March, English in Norway

A kidney stone is the last thing you need,
especially when you have just arrived.

One of my major concerns on relocating with young children to a new country was, of course, the quality of medical care — would it be up to scratch should the need arise? One of my dearest hopes was that we would never have to find out. On moving to Stavanger, Norway, I discovered that, as so often in my life, my concerns were as ill-founded as my hopes were confounded.

Nine days after arrival I could find my way unaided, or with the help of the local *Kartbok*, to the British School and to a supermarket. I also said 'hello' to three people. In my husband's judgement I was fully settled and could handle the house and children while he went offshore for two weeks. Never mind the fact that he would be away longer than my feet had been on Norwegian soil.

As I waved goodbye at the heliport I felt a twist in my stomach. Strange, I thought, we decided long before to halt the production of more offspring, Seventeen hours of hard labour, an attempt at ventouse delivery without pain relief and a Caesarean section had heralded the birth of our first child five years before. Could relocation to Norway, with its scenic fjords and majestic mountains, have been the catalyst required for a spot of recklessness? I belched. Possibly not.

Driving off manfully on the wrong side of the road and clutching the wheel with every spasm of pain, I cursed those strange dumplings I'd been talked into eating and remembered that the best way to cure a tummy bug is to starve it out. My resolve held for 36 hours until I was no longer sure which was causing the greater pain — hunger or upset stomach — and recklessly ate a dry water biscuit. Almost immediately, I was struck to my knees on the kitchen floor while attempting to decipher Norwegian cooking instructions for unfamiliar fish cakes for the children's supper. Not surprisingly a migraine jumped on the bandwagon and I limped off to bed.

After two sleepless nights writhing on the relative comfort of the heated bathroom floor, I — stalwart as I am, offshore widow, experienced at coping with disasters alone — realised that even I had never been this alone before. I was forced, for the first time in my life to give in and request that my husband do the unthinkable — put his family before the company and come home.

Much to my relief he was on the next helicopter and home within three and a half hours. Much to his relief, since he seemed under the misapprehension that he had been summoned from duty by a wimpish migraine, which would not go down at all well with the company. And 36 hours later I was admitted to the emergency room at Stavanger General Hospital.

As my only previous hospitalisation had occurred in a British Maternity Hospital I was certainly not prepared for two of the Norwegian admissions procedures. Firstly, I was presented with a perfectly decent, perfectly comfortable hospital gown — no back opening leaving an embarrassing two inch gap from neck to rear, not so starched that every movement resulted in painful chafing. It was even a pretty colour and decorated with flowers, I stared at it in disbelief before being met with my second shock. I was requested to take my temperature by a nurse who was aghast when I started to place the thermometer in my mouth. She struggled to find the correct English quickly enough: "Bottom!" she finally said triumphantly. "You put it in your bottom." My husband and children brightened visibly; this would liven things up. I stared at the door. I wanted to go home; no, not just up the road to the rented house in Røyneberg, but real home. Suddenly a chafing hospital gown seemed a small price to pay for the luxury of a British thermometer tucked comfortably under my tongue. But the deed had to be done.

Once the formalities were complete and it seemed unlikely that further entertaining diversions would be on offer, my yawning husband and children went home, leaving me to await removal to the ward. The strangeness of being alone in a foreign hospital, still unsure what was wrong with me and what might be done to me, was alleviated by a comfortingly familiar touch. I was left lying in an ante room for two hours before a nurse looked in and said in surprise, "Are you still here? I think they've forgotten about you." I smiled nostalgically. Apart from scent, it could have been home.

The next two days passed in a whirl of new experiences. I was required to urinate into a receptacle suitably sized and shaped for ladies. A nurse unpacked my belongings for me into my locker, and expressed surprise at my nightdress, towel and toiletries. I discovered why, when I was presented with a clean nightdress, towels and a sort of boxer shorts, (sympathetically marked 'small'). In addition, there were soap and shampoo in the bathrooms, pillows on the bed and clean cutlery at every meal. Previously, if more than one pillow was required then it had to be brought from home. I would also have been issued with a set of cutlery on admission for which I was responsible until my discharge. I took the abundant personal supplies in Norway to mean that inhabitants of one of the wealthiest countries in the world don't need to steal.

And as for the nurses, they were in abundant supply too. Quite often, in our pleasant four-bedded ward, there were more nurses than patients. They brought drinks, picked up magazines, plumped the pillows, chatted and reprimanded me for not buzzing when I needed them. Instead of waking us at six for a brief prodding before leaving us blinking in the bright lights of another long, tedious hospital day, they woke us leisurely around eight.

However, all good things come to an end. My condition improved and it was decided that I had passed a kidney stone. I had been the only person in the hospital without blonde hair and had unwittingly killed half the patients on life support machines because I had been unable to understand the warnings about not using mobile phones, but it had been a wonderful two days and quite wasted on a poorly person. I resolved that next time things got rough I would stage a neat collapse outside the doors.

Hospitalisation in a foreign country can be a traumatic experience. My husband had been faced with the fact that his children go to school and require clean, ironed clothes and a packed lunch to do so. Sometimes it's harder on the relatives.

When not helping others make an impact with their written words through her proofreading and editing work, Linda is working on a novel and family history.

www.goodenglishcompany.com

Travelling with the Bitch
Apple Gidley, Anglo-Australian

Moving our pets can bring out the worst in us.

I rarely lay down ultimatums as I find they have a tendency to backfire. This time I did. "If I go, the other bitch goes too," I told my long-suffering spouse.

He nodded, resigned to travelling from America to Africa in the company of two recalcitrant females, both whining and howling at different stages of the journey.

The day of departure dawned hellish hot and the check-in staff at American Airlines did all they humanly could to make the transfer of an animal of dubious origins as difficult as possible. This despite the plethora of paperwork I had at hand. Passport, check; rabies certificate, check, though I thought that a bit rich considering our destination; bortadella certificate, check, though I wondered how many dogs would be on the same plane to a miniscule, despotic West African country. I was pretty sure I could count them on one finger.

Paperwork finally done we waved our black and white hybrid off. Her indignation at being caged precluded her from waving back. As she disappeared into the confines of the truck charged with delivering her to the plane, her whines changed to howls. It was not a happy start to twenty-four hours of intercontinental hell.

The first stage of our trip was short; Houston to Dallas. It was the next leg that worried me most; the transfer of said dog from one plane to another. What if they left her in the initial plane? What if they left her in the truck? What if she needed to pee? What if she ran away while peeing? What if they forgot to turn the air-conditioning on in the hold of the next plane? It was here the forbearance of my husband was sorely tested as he attempted to assuage my anxiety.

I was distracted for a moment as I turned to glare at the large, sweaty and over-burdened woman following me up the aisle as she clipped my heels yet again with the sharp edge of her push-in-front carry on.

Being the shorter member of our partnership I was urged into the middle seat where I spent a couple of moments organising my affairs. Book, glasses, *Hello!* magazine, water. My patience was admirable. I waited until the vast majority of the travelling public were in situ and then urged my husband to flag down a stewardess.

"Do you mean a flight attendant?"

"You know exactly what I mean. Just grab one please."

It was here the real inadequacies of the flight staff came to the fore. Their ability to not see an initially politely raised hand and later a frantically waving arm and hand as they slammed their way down the aisles, pushing and shoving bulging bags into the confines of the overhead lockers, was astounding.

"Do you think they are all myopic?" I muttered as another turned on her heel as she neared our section.

"Just busy," my husband placated me.

"Rubbish. Not one of them has actually helped anyone with bags, or seats," I replied as my waving reached fever pitch. "Excuse me," I said, now standing.

"Yes?"

"Would you mind checking that my dog has been loaded in the temperature-controlled hold please?" I asked with a near perfect smile, even if it did not quite reach my eyes.

"All cargo is aboard," the woman, whose uniform strained across an ample bottom, said. "Please sit down, we are about to close the doors and leave the jetway."

Now I knew that wasn't true because I could see stragglers still stumbling along the aisle on the long trek to the back of the aircraft. I smiled again.

"I'm sure it has, but would you please just double check for me, I am anxious."

"Ma'am, please sit. I have told you, all cargo is aboard," the bitch in blue replied. "Now please sit down."

I remained standing. "My dog is live cargo; not exactly the same as luggage is it? Now please just check for me."

"You have to sit."

"Not until you have checked," I countered.

My husband touched my arm tentatively. "She'll be okay you know."

"I just want to know she is actually on the plane. Look at them all, standing around doing bugger all. It is not a huge ask."

Another woman in blue, this one slightly less large and a little less aged, approached. "Ma'am, you really must sit down, we are about to start moving."

"I am not sitting down until you have confirmed my dog is aboard. Is it really that difficult to check for me?"

"Soright hun," said a voice behind me, "I'd wanna know too."

"Yeah," said another from across the aisle. I smiled my gratitude at their understanding. My husband sat resigned. I stood defiant as I watched the hostess' jagged walk to the front of the plane scream irritation.

Her passage was thwarted by a stocky man in khaki and as they danced the tight-squeeze-tango I felt a pang for the passenger faced with a blue-clad behind.

The man continued his amble down the aisle. He checked a piece of wilted paper and approached. "Are you Miss Meg's mom?" he asked.

"Yes, that's me."

"Jes' wan'd to letya know, she's jes fine. Might pretty dawg ya got there. Gave 'er another ice cube. She'll be fine."

"Oh thank you so much." If I could have reached him I would have kissed him.

"No problem ma'am. Y'all 'ave a good flight now," he said as he turned and made his way back along the plane.

I bounced into the hardness of the seat, buckled up and smiled at my husband.

"Thank God, now we can relax," he said squeezing my hand.

"You happy now?" tossed the hostess, as she retreated to her seat ready for take off, and before her next arduous task of dispensing beef or chicken.

"Yes, thank you," I replied sweetly.

Apple Gidley writes on expatriate issues based on her experiences as a lifetime global nomad, living and working in Africa, Asia, Europe and the US. In 2012 she published her memoir, Expat Life Slice by Slice.

www.expatapple.com
Blog: www.my.telegraph.co.uk/applegidley
Twitter: @expatapple

Inflight

"The nearest city was 50 miles away and a two hour drive from our isolated compound where 25 families lived. We were not all expatriates and we all socialized together. We had no community services, just a coconut grove, with palms on one side and the ocean on the other."

Colleen Macdonald in Trinidad

"Even when I was settled, it never felt 'ordinary'. There was always something bizarre or unusual going on — like finding an alligator in the back garden or going to a rodeo."

Alice Hurley in the United States of America

"I had learned the rules of expatriate society and how to fit in so that relationships with people were improved."

Susan Valentine in The Sultanate of Oman.

"I could remember my local cashpoint number but not the one back 'home'. I no longer needed to take the street plan with me and knew the whereabouts of all the public lavatories."

Sarah Burton in Paris

"I spent 13 years there but never felt really settled. They say that you are not truly accepted until a Swiss family invites you for a cheese fondue. With a cheese fondue you all dip your wooden sticks with speared bread cube into a communal pot. Then you put the cheese-covered bread in your mouth. Then you spear a new piece of bread and begin again. This is very unhygienic and very un-Swiss. Ergo only family and very close friends are allowed to be fellow-dippers. Needless to say I was never invited."

Paul Cleary in Switzerland

"Being settled is the feeling that you know where you are, who you are and where you are going, what you want and where to get it. It happens one morning when you wake up and realise you have overcome culture shock and can throw yourself wholeheartedly at the day."

Christine Yates in Germany

"I had come to accept the bureaucracy and the endless paperwork."

Mark Eadie in The Netherlands

"Our research has shown that it takes six years to truly settle in."

Anne Copeland,
Intercultural Exchange Institute, USA

Tales of a Tomboy in Tokyo
By Laura Kline, American in Japan

An unusual 'culture bump'

I used to be a tomboy. But what is a tomboy anyway? The Cambridge dictionary says it's: "a girl who acts and dresses like a boy, liking noisy, physical activities." My mom tried to dress me as a girl. But I loved my army shorts with zillions of pockets until she bought me frilly underpants to go underneath. Of course, I hacked off that ridiculous pink lace. Tomboys can be extremely talented with sewing scissors, even at age five.

As an adolescent, I was so flat, when I finally got a training bra, it fit better backwards. Finally, at thirty-three, I bagged my boyishness and relocated to Fukushima prefecture in northern Japan. But just when I thought I'd given up life as a tomboy, the land of the rising sun had a huge *surpriizu* (surprise) for me: — everyone thought I was a guy.

Okay, I had swimmers' shoulders — so impractical for kimonos. And I did have short hair, but I made up for it by wearing make-up and flashy earrings. Besides, I had sprouted real boobs, so I could safely wear my bra forwards like everyone else. Yet despite these womanly decorations, as soon as the Japanese spotted me, they usually referred to me as a *dansei* (boy).

The worst part was when I had to go to the *o-tearai* (toilet).

As if on cue, Japanese women entering a public *o-tearai* freaked out. One look at me and they ran to the *o-tearai* door to check the pink kanji symbol that read *onna* (women). Then they glanced at me again, screwed up their faces, and uttered: "*Are?*" (what the...?). Their heads swiveled towards the door again, then at me. "*Are? Nan da be?*" (what the heck?) Then they ran out, certain they had entered the men's room by mistake.

Embarrassingly enough, this *o-tearai* ritual occurred daily during my stay in Japan. As a thirty-something woman, I felt perturbed. I had moved to Japan after my femininity had blossomed. If only the Japanese could have figured that out. Japan has an extremely role-defined culture, with a distinct notion of *sekshee* (sexy). Girls wear frilly, pink clothes with lace, and even pigtails, even in their late-twenties. As a student struggling to finish my dissertation, however, I wasn't trying to impress anybody with curls and crimps, fluffy folds and flowers. That's why every time I peed, I was peeved, humiliated by this cross-cultural gender identification mix-up.

I gazed in the mirror each day to reassure myself. "I'm not even remotely 'butch,' they're just ultra-feminine," I decided. Even salarywomen (business women) split my eardrums with unnaturally high-pitched voices. They were constantly brushing their long, silky hair, painting their delicate nails, and red geisha lips. They carried parasols, wore white gloves, and displayed picture-perfect, powdered faces. So I gave up trying to look like them. I knew if I tried, they'd think I was in drag. Actually, I did, and they did.

But life went on. I finished my dissertation, defended it in Japanese, and got my Ph.D. On my last day in Japan, my mom, who had come for graduation, watched my bags as I slipped off to the *o-tearai* at Narita airport.

I was pulling up my panties when... I heard an older man grunt "*Dansei da.*" (It's a boy.)

An older woman retorted, "*Iie, chigau. Josei da.*" (No, wrong, it's a girl.)

Not only was this in Japanese, but in dialect — my Fukushima dialect. I shivered. Throngs of people instantly gathered outside my stall. Excited voices chirped as I, the *gaijin* (foreigner), stood half-naked, huddling in the loo. Nobody guessed I could understand them, since most *gaijins* don't speak fluent Japanese; and certainly not Fukushima-ben dialect... But *gaijins* who just earned a Ph.D. in Japanese do. The voices continued:

"It's got short hair."

"But I saw boobs!... Big ones..." I knew only too well whom they were discussing. More voices chimed in.

"You're wrong, it's a boy!"

"No, it's a girl!"

"Wrong, I saw it. It's a boy."

I felt stupid, scrunched over the low, oblong bowl on the floor — typical of traditional Japan — trying to figure out how to exit my stall. While I listened to the crowd debating my gender, images of my mom nervously checking her watch tortured me. I felt nauseous. Beads of sweat littered my face as precious minutes ticked by. I imagined missed flights and my mom growing hysterical.

Then it hit me; did I want to spend my last day in Japan cowering over a toilet bowl?

Heck no! I was a *Dokutaa* (Doctor) now, and I deserved some respect! I would teach these people a lesson they'd never forget. Besides, I had already turned in my *gaijin* card and couldn't return as a resident. So, I thrust open the stall door to face dozens of curious elderly faces staring at me — the sexless gaijin — towering over them. Their mouths dropped open.

I dipped my hands under the faucet, slicked my hair back, and exclaimed in the most formal Japanese I could muster: "*Sumimasen desu ga, oppai ga arimasu. Desu kara, josei desu!*" (Excuse me, it has breasts. Therefore, it's a girl!). Then I stuck out my breasts and paraded out of my stall.

Excited voices behind me exclaimed: "*Josei da!*" (It's a girl!), as I went through the crowd. My mom, oblivious to my turmoil in the *o-tearai*, casually exclaimed: "Whatever took you so long dear?"

Now, back in Europe, I don't have to pile on make-up and earrings, nor jut out my breasts to prove I'm a woman. Men call me Madame and open doors for me. A few months ago, however, as I got off a train in Brussels, I heard a shrill: "Monsieur, Monsieur!" (Sir!). Sure enough, a young Japanese woman stood clutching my umbrella.

"*Domo arigato gozaimashita,*" I thanked her, in my highest-pitched voice. Skipping away from the platform, I recalled my final, triumphant day in Japan and muttered: "*Josei da!*"

Laura Kline resides in Belgium and enjoys sharing humorous anecdotes from her expat experiences. Note: she finally stopped cutting the lace off her underwear.

A Belly Full of Laughs!
Jae De Wylde, British-Dutch in Dubai

Jae De Wylde lived and danced in Dubai.
Here she recalls her most cringe-worthy moment…

I stood shaking on the edge of the stage as her fabulous performance drew to a close. Follow that, I thought. Or maybe I can just sneak away and…

"And now please welcome Jae De Wylde, all the way from the UK…" The ballroom filled with my music and I heard a rustle of anticipation from the crowd. Someone prodded me from behind.

"Jae, it's you. You're on."

Yes, I know, I wanted to say, but please don't make me. How the hell can I follow that?

It was my own fault. I had listened to the encouragement from my pupils and mentor. Of course I should dance in the festival… why wouldn't I? They had been so lovely, used words like 'inspirational' about my teaching. I had been happily lulled into self-belief. But at that moment I could think of a million reasons, top of the list being that I was at least twice the age of any other dancer and at most half as supple. My daughter's words screamed in my head. "Are you sure you want to do this, Mum? After all, you're a belly dance instructor, not a belly dancer." Oh shit.

I had been so lucky, no blessed, with where we landed in Dubai. As soon as I knew we were going to live in the Middle East I decided to add belly dance to my repertoire. Martin was teaching Art and Design and there, directly behind his school was a ballet and belly dance studio... as if plonked there just for me. Thank you God, Allah and the Belly Dance Fairy. I was completely captivated by the fabulous moves and exotic music and my progress was fast. Soon I began teaching — yes, teaching — at the studio. It was all good. Until that moment.

That they put the very best dancer in the show in the slot before me was either bad luck or a sort of sabotage with the organisers deciding they needed the perfect foil for the lovely sexy-pink, über-young, back-bending, all-shaking creature — and I was it.

No choice. Slap on a smile, keep the crows feet well behind the veil, shimmy fast and hope the stage lights would hide not highlight the bingo wings.

You know when you are it and you get that hopeless feeling that you are never going to win and that the game will never end. Well, that's how it was up there on the stage. My three minute music lasted at least 30 and as I held my arms high in my last pose I just wanted the whole thing not to have happened. I felt so old, so sun-leathered and like my belly was one fat crinkle, like the crisps with the extra bumps to soak up the grease.

The *compère* was thanking me and it was time to exit. Hurrah!

I wrapped my veil around me, grabbed my clothes and made for the door. Maybe I could find a loo to change in rather than face the superior 20-somethings in the dressing room.

"Excuse me, Ms Jae."

I recognised this guy. An Arabic guy, he was a sort of belly dance bodyguard who tagged along with the organisers. He was youngish and pretty handsome in that dusky Arabian prince kind of way.

"Yes?" I was in no mood for a chat.

"Ms Jae, you are not past."

"What?"

"You are not past, Ms Jae."

"*It*. You are not past *it* is what you mean. You have to use the pronoun," I spat.

"No, Ms Jae, you don't understand. You are not passed." He handed me a visitor's pass. I had arrived way before showtime and had been in the dressing room by the time anything official had been set up.

The event had already been one big chunk of humiliation — and it had just got worse. If I had sat factor-free in the burning desert sun for 12 hours, my face would not have been a deeper shade of red.

"I..."

"No wor-r-ries," the Arabic 'r' rolled repeatedly on his tongue as the smirk spread across his face.

I held my veil firmly across my 50-year-old bosom, snatched the pass from his outstretched hand and turned towards the door.

"No worries, Ms Jae. You come to my suite and you will see that you are not past *it*."

Did I turn back or acknowledge the comment? No, of course I didn't. But the weight of being the oldest dancer in town lifted slightly, and I couldn't help the curl of my lips.

Maybe there's fire in my belly yet!

Half Dutch, Jae De Wylde is a linguist and has lived in France, Germany, Spain and Dubai, where she completed her first novel, The Thinking Tank.

www.jaedewylde.com
Blog: www.Life'scrappystuff.wordpress.com
Twitter: @jaedewylde
Facebook: www.facebookcom/JaeDeWylde

Partying all the Way to a Cultural Gaffe
Christina Louise, Dane in China

The horror of the Christmas party in a strange land

"We would like to invite you to our party on the 26th of December. Will you come?" the two smiley Chinese female students asked me when I opened the door of my hotel room which had become my home for a year.

The year was 1993, and I had been living in China for two months, working as an English teacher at the Agricultural University of Tai'an in the Province of Shandong. As one of only 15 foreign faces in a city with more than three hundred thousand inhabitants, I felt almost like a celebrity when walking down the streets. People would wave and shout "Hello!" when I was out shopping and point at me while speaking to each other. If I stopped in the street for any longer than five minutes I would immediately draw a crowd of curious people, observing my every move and discussing what I was doing.

"Thank you so much, I would love to come," I replied.

The two students clapped with delight at my accepting their invitation.

"Will you prepare something that you can perform at the party?" they asked. I replied that I would do my best. "It will almost be like a Christmas Party since it is on the 26th of December," they added.

In the first couple of months living in Tai'an I had already been invited to many parties: ballroom dancing, end of semester and English practising parties. My short Chinese partying experience had involved groups of approximately 10 people around a circular table consuming tea, sunflower seeds and fruit while actively chatting with each other. Each guest would take turns standing up to perform something they had prepared such as a song, a poem, telling a story or showing a particular skill. I found it curious that while one person performed, the other participants would continue their chatter and mindlessly clap when the performance was finished.

I noted the date of the invitation and spent a total of ten seconds deciding that my performance would be a song: *Jingle Bells*. This seemed an appropriate act that had a good chance of winning some popularity as it also had Chinese lyrics.

A week later, the two Chinese students came back to visit. They were preparing a dance act which involved running around on tiptoes, jumping on each other's backs and making graceful movements with their hands. To give me the full effect they hummed the music along with their impromptu performance in the hotel corridor outside my room door. I told them they were great and wondered why they were putting so much effort into preparing a piece that would only be seen by chattering distracted partygoers.

The students asked me how my act was coming along

and I told them about my idea of singing Jingle Bells. Puzzled, they asked me if I had a backing tape and I assured them that I was a good singer and would not need one.

What happened next was something that I could not have been more unprepared for. Despite having lived in many countries and knowing about cultural misunderstandings, this one caught me completely off guard.

As convened, on the evening of the 26th of December, my two Chinese friends picked me up in time for the party. I immediately realized that my jeans were a mismatch with their beautiful gowns so I decided to quickly change into my black slacks before leaving the hotel.

We walked over to a black building I had never noticed before at one end of the university campus. As the doors opened I was standing in a gigantic auditory hall with room for a few thousand spectators. At the front was a professional stage with heavy curtains, backdrops, lighting and sound system.

The room was filled to the brim. I was ushered to the seat of honour on the third row right behind the Mayor of the city. Seconds later the show started with the most exquisite performances I had ever seen: graceful petite dancers in colourful silk dresses, young athletic men performing military dances, fantastic singers, musicians and backing tapes. My translator told me that this show was marking a unique occasion: the one hundredth anniversary of the birth of Mao Zedong.

I felt sick to my stomach at the thought of getting up to sing *Jingle Bells* in the middle of this enchanting show. My naive expectation of 10 people mindlessly clapping at my performance had suddenly turned into a living nightmare. I wondered how I could escape and asked my Chinese friends if it was okay that I didn't perform. They politely explained that this was not an option since my name was on the programme.

My mind was blank and my hands were sweaty as I walked up the stairs onto the stage. In panic I asked one of my friends to join me on the stage to translate for me. In the moment, I decided to turn my performance into a sing along exercise with the audience; hoping that through personal participation my lacklustre performance would be better received.

Microphone in hand and with hundreds of eyes looking at me my voice rang through a silent room.

"As you know, in my country it is Christmas time at the moment."

The hall broke into loud clapping. Then, my friend translated my sentence which was met with complete silence.

"So, I want to sing a Christmas song for you called *Jingle Bells*. I believe most of you know it, so please sing along or clap along if you know it."

Loud applause broke out once more. And after the translation, there was total silence again.

With a completely blank mind, I started to sing. I am a good singer, so I was in tune and would have sounded really great if I had been under my shower. Once my song died down, you could have heard a pin drop. Through the fog of my discomfort I felt disappointed that I did not have a single participant singing along with me and in a desperate attempt to foster a spirit of togetherness I decided to give it one more try. I spoke to the audience again and told them that I did not hear them sing along last time and urged them to sing along this time. The strange pattern of applause after each sentence before the translator got a chance to speak continued. I launched into yet another rendition of Jingle Bells, which again only resulted in complete silence from the audience.

I thanked them all for their attention and quickly walked off the stage. My two friends hugged me and told me I was great and gave me a notebook as a gift to remember the event by.

To this day, I still have the notebook. Surprisingly it has become a memento of one of the most embarrassing moments in my life.

Did I learn something from it? Yes, two things: If you are invited to a social event make sure you know what the event is, the appropriate etiquette for the occasion, and what is expected of you. Secondly, if you are in a country where you cannot read poster announcements, ask someone to translate them for you.

A serial expat, Christina Louise is Danish by birth, grew up in France, lived for a decade in the UK and has now settled in Utrecht in The Netherlands. She specializes in coaching women who are juggling life and work and writes about her journey towards a happy and balanced life. She maintains an inspirational blog at www.christinalouise.net.

www.christinalouise.net
Blog: www.christinalouise.net/blog
Twitter: @jugglersjourney
Facebook: www.facebook.com/ChristinaLouise.net

Falling Rain
Debbie Fletcher, English in Spain

Because sometimes everything does go wrong

I'm beginning to understand how Noah felt.

Last weekend was fiesta weekend for Bullas the *Fiesta de San Marcos*. The saint after whom our overgrown yak puppy was named, given that he (the dog, not the saint), was foisted upon me four years ago at the very same *fiesta*.

On Saturday, the rain proved to be one of those uninvited and unwelcome thick-skinned guests that refuse to take the hint and leave. It fell relentlessly throughout the afternoon, soaking through the canopy of pine branches at the La Rafa camping centre (the focus of *fiesta* activity) to fall heavily onto the ground below and all things set upon it. During the *San Marcos* celebrations, this includes many groups of people (*peñas*) all laboriously stoking bonfires under huge paella pans for a communal rice-and-unmentionable-things feast.

This year the pathetic wisps of smoke bore witness to the dampness of spirit and body of the participants —

a sad contrast to the buzz and colour, the aromas and, well, the *warmth* we experienced at this same event last year.

The evening proved little better at the outset and downright unpleasant at its close. I met up with some friends in town for a fiesta drink, but alas many people had eschewed further outings for the day given the general air of sogginess that pervaded all things, so the evening was fairly subdued. We called it a day fairly early on, given that we would be up early-ish for the Sunday parade, and I drove home. To a blacked-out *finca*.

The incessant rain had obviously found its way into some connection or other, probably in the outside lighting circuit, and had thrown the circuit breaker for all external power.

Now John, my husband, is a gadget merchant. If there is a gizmo to be had for this, or a widget to be had for that, then John's the man to want it. We therefore have electric gates. Which don't work when the power is summarily cut.

So I am parked up in the car on the outside of the *finca* with no other illumination than the headlights shining upon the pair of staunchly immovable six-foot wrought iron gates (with spikes on top and no pedestrian entrance), which sit across the top of a steep drive down to the house level from the *camino*.

Along the left-hand edge of the descending drive there is a wall that supports the *camino* — starting at about two foot high at the top of the drive, this grows to a good eleven foot high at the bottom of the drive. And it is topped by a six-foot chain link fence, which extends along its length from the gates, ending at a metal post that coincides with the end of the wall.

As I sat there gazing helplessly upon the scene, the

dogs below realised that I had returned home and that, further, they could in all probability play the sympathy card and thus elicit a morsel of extra grub, and so began to howl. I had at that point reached the conclusion that my only way in was to make my way along the bank on the outside of the chain-link fence to the end of the wall, swing round the end post and then proceed back again on the inside of the fence along the top of the wall to the gates and thence to the top of the drive.

Good plan, Stan. Except that I was undertaking this venture with glaring headlights behind me, which rendered me unable to see much given that, I was casting a hulking great shadow across my own path. Oh, and also except that I was shod with the most ridiculous pair of stiletto-heeled ankle boots. So, by the time I'd got to the end of the fence on the outbound leg of the journey, my feet were totally caked in thick mud, such that my boots were giving a fair impression of concrete wellies, and my heels looked like the orders spike in an exceedingly busy restaurant.

So, as I executed stage two of my brilliant plan and swung round the post at the end of the fence with my left foot, I couldn't actually feel the bank below my right one. Probably, in fact, because it wasn't there, and my right foot, therefore dropped into nothingness.

This gave rise to two things: one, the inside of my right knee scraped painfully down the end of the wall (and I am sitting nursing a five-inch bruise as a result as I write this); and two, the only way I could stop myself from plummeting backwards down the eleven-foot drop onto the (concrete) drive, was to grab the chain-link fence and swing.

As I was clinging to the fence, the end post groaned, and moved.

I still just about had my left foot on the top of the wall, but my chin was almost resting on my knee. My right leg was dangling into the pitch-black void being no help whatsoever. The fence, with its end post no longer fully vertical, had slackened, and flashing through my mind was the fact that John was likely either to kill me for breaking the fence, or for breaking my neck.

Suffice to say, that I did manage to haul myself back up again without further movement of the fence post, although I did have to sacrifice all the nails on my left hand. I then had to make my way slowly back atop the wall towards the gate on the inside of the flapping chain-link, shaking like a jelly in an earthquake. The clamour from the dogs, indignant that they were apparently being ignored, was climbing in direct proportion to my lack of muscle control, and to add insult to injury I was being blinded by the headlights that were by then in front of me. But I did, I'm pleased to report, remain somehow on top of the wall for the rest of the venture.

Once I'd managed to achieve the gate end of the wall, I dropped the last two foot onto the drive, and promptly slid down the slope as the mud-encrusted boots hit the wet concrete surface. The downward movement was arrested only when contact was made between the surface of the drive and my left bum cheek, upon which has subsequently flourished yet another bruise.

The rest needs no further description, and, having gained entry to the house and reset the circuit breaker, the car and I were safely back where we belonged in no time at all.

The dogs were placated with cheese and I consoled myself with chocolate.

And yes, John is prematurely grey, bless him.

Deborah Fletcher is the author of Bitten by Spain. *Born south-east England, 1958. Died, 2003. Reborn south-east Spain, 2003. Mediterranean childhood progressing with expected turbulence, but looking forward to teens this time round.*

www.bittenbyspain.com
Blog: www.bittenbyspain.com

Divine Intervention and a Wine Festival in Chile

Reina van Nieuwkerk-Rácz,
Dutch-Hungarian in Chile

How far can you expand your comfort zone?

A previous engagement had prevented the Dutch ambassador's wife from attending the *Vendimia* at *Curicó*, Chile's most prestigious annual wine festival. She had been asked to be the Madrina or Godmother, whose duty was to officially open the festivities.

The invitation was duly passed on to the deputy ambassador, a bit of a wine buff, who readily accepted the invitation on his wife's behalf and upon hearing that she would also be expected to give *just a little* speech, had assured the ambassador that she'd be thrilled. And that's how I ended up in the car on my way to *Curicó*: furious at my husband for saying yes without first asking me; and terrified about having to give a speech to a couple of thousand people in a language I most certainly had not mastered.

A local police escort was to accompany us into *Curicó* but when nobody showed up at the appointed time it became evident that they had forgotten us. We had decided to move on and rely on our own sense of direction, when we suddenly saw a policeman standing in the middle of the *autostrada* pointing at us with one hand and waving the other back and forth frantically, indicating us to stop. Our police escort, surely?

My husband greeted the policeman cheerfully through the open window, but instead of a friendly response the man sternly demanded to see our car papers and asked where we were headed. It was quite obvious this was not our escort. This was a random police check and we'd been caught speeding!

"We're from the Dutch embassy and on our way to the wine festival, actually I have the *Madrina* in the car with me," my husband answered rather pleased he'd been asked.

When he also pointed out that we'd been waiting for a police escort that had never shown up, our unfriendly policeman nervously started mumbling into his walkie-talkie. A crackly reply had him staring up the road and sure enough there they were; two white specks on big white motorbikes. With a stiff salute and wishing us a '*muy, muy buen dia*' our now jovial policeman waved us goodbye.

We entered *Curicó* with one motorway policeman leading the way whilst his colleague followed behind. Clearly the entire town was at the festival because the roads were completely deserted, and we felt a bit conspicuous being escorted through what seemed a ghost town. Nevertheless, we arrived safely at our first appointment of the day, the Robles Wine Co-operation, where the renowned and very charming winemaker, Miguel Torres, greeted us and introduced us to the newly elected Harvest Queen who was in full regalia: white ball gown, glittering crown and satin sash, professing her to be *La Reina*, the queen. Ironically, Reina happens also to be my first name, in Dutch though, without the royal connotations!

We had a most informative tour of the wine facilities after which Mr Torres asked the two *Reinas* and my husband to step into an open horse drawn carriage that was elaborately decorated with fresh flowers. We clip-clopped through the empty streets and suddenly there they were — thousands of people had gathered in the town square.

A large tent had been constructed in the middle of the square facing a huge podium where the most traditional dance of Chile, the *cueca*, was being performed. Next a local priest blessed the new harvest and the wine and then Mr Torres asked me to escort him to the podium, giving me a quick wink for courage. As he put on his reading glasses and started to unfold a piece of paper with his speech on it, I realized to my utter horror that I had left mine in my handbag! There wasn't much I could do, TV cameras were aimed at us and so I slowly edged towards Mr Torres, little by little until I was hidden behind him. Fortunately, my husband was staring at me wondering what on God's earth I was doing, which enabled me to quickly communicate to him what I needed and to my relief he understood and placed the paper in my hand, just as Mr Torres was stepping aside to make room for me in front of the microphone. I read my short speech slowly, carefully articulating. I declared that this was going to be the best wine year and the crowd went wild; they were clapping and cheering as if I'd just announced that Chile had won the World Cup! I had done it and lived. With the official part of the festival over, we were asked to walk amongst the crowd and visit some of the stands.

"The people like to take photos of the *Madrina*," one of the organizers had told me and so my husband and I walked from wine stand to wine stand, posing with anyone who wanted to take a picture. The local radio wanted a short interview, my husband obliged, local newspapers wanted a few words of wisdom from the *Madrina* or her husband, again he obliged. The time ticked by and we soon realized that we should start heading out to the Torres winery where a lunch for about four hundred people was about to take place and we were the guests of honour! We hurried to the courtesy lounge just off the main square, where someone would be waiting to take us to the vineyard, which is located a couple of kilometers out of town. But the room was empty. Not again! We'd been forgotten. We were stuck, our car was parked at the *Robles* winery and the lunch was supposed to start in about fifteen minutes.

Finding a taxi, let alone a taxi driver who wasn't completely inebriated at a wine festival is about as easy as finding a chicken with teeth, so, you can imagine our relief when we stumbled upon a familiar face.

It was the *padre* who had performed the blessing at the opening of the festival. When we explained to him what had happened he was horrified.

"*Qué* horror, but no worry I also going to ze lunch, I take you but first we must get to ze church," he exclaimed lifting his eyes towards the heavens and crossing himself.

By now we had assembled a bit of a crowd, and the Chief of Police came by to have a look at what was going on. When the kindly *padre* explained our dilemma it was quickly decided that he would bring us all to the church in his police car. We were all piled into the back of the dark blue Fiat, and with tires smoking tore off towards the church. Upon arrival the priest jumped out of the car, holding onto his wide brimmed hat and with robes flying in all directions hurried to a side door re-emerging seconds later through two large barn doors, scattering a couple of terrified chickens. Soon we heard an engine revving and a sky blue Fiat 500 slowly backed out of the barn, with the frantic *padre* waving at us to get in.

Thanks to divine intervention, we made it to the lunch in the nick of time, plank gassing all the way to the winery where the heavenly blue Fiat screeched to an abrupt halt, spitting distance from the lunch guests enjoying their aperitifs *al fresco.*

Reina van Nieuwkerk-Rácz is a British educated Dutch-Hungarian. Having lived in eleven countries she has returned to Holland, working as a freelance writer and editor of The Underground.

www.theunderground.com
Blog: www.expatcalidocious.com
Twitter: @xpatcalidocious
Facebook: www.facebook.com/Expatcalidocious

Dinner Party Disasters
Jo Parfitt (with thanks to Australian Elise Allen)

Entertaining can be entertaining

You've been in your new country of residence for a few months now. Met a few people along the way and it's time to cement some of those relationships. You decide to have a party.

In our ten years abroad we have thrown many dinner parties, supper parties, leaving parties, children's parties, family sized lunches and brunches. We have enjoyed the excellent company of so many nationalities that I have lost count. Customs and cultures intermingle on the expatriate network. Non Chinese will gaily tackle chopsticks, dainty Brits will eat with their fingers and without serviettes and even the French don't seem to care if the pudding comes before the cheese. Such cosmopolitan dining has made our time abroad rich, interesting and hugely entertaining. Friendships have been cemented with more laughs than can be found in a bottle of Moet. Some of our best friends are Dutch too. A comment that will make sense when you learn what happened to Elise.

When Elise and Rod first went to Holland from their native Australia, they discovered that a dinner party was a highly complicated affair.

Soon after their arrival in The Hague, they decided to throw a casual house warming party for Elise's colleagues, inviting their guests to arrive at eight p.m. and to bring a bottle.

To their horror, the guests all arrived on time. Elise wore her jeans. The guests wore nice dresses and suits. They all brought her huge bunches of flowers and chocolates. No one had brought any wine. She dumped the growing piles of flowers on the draining board in the kitchen and went back to Rod, who was wrestling with the cheese fondue.

They soon discovered that Dutch cheese was not meant for a fondue. The Gouda refused to become anything other than a solid yellow ball that floated round in a sea of white wine. Rod served the guests with their first drinks and then invited them to help themselves. They didn't, which was fortunate really because there wasn't much anyway.

Things went from bad to worse. The fondue was inedible. The guests ate nothing, sat uncomfortably round the coffee table and scowled in the direction of the forgotten flowers and chocolates. In desperation Elise offered to make some coffee and everyone brightened up. She had bought a really expensive jar especially for the evening, but no one touched a drop. Eventually, the evening ended and Elise and Rod flopped into bed not sure whether to laugh or cry.

However, the next week at work, word had reached Elise's boss. He called her into his office and asked her to close the door. He went on to suggest that she and Rod attend a week long cultural awareness course.

They learned a lot. Firstly, they were expected to only

invite people to dinner if they had enough wine available. A good hostess should have as many vases as she invites guests. Flowers should be fussed over and arranged immediately. Dinner should be served at a dining table. Chocolates should be offered with the coffee, which should not, on any account, be instant.

Relieved that they were unlikely to make quite so many dreadful errors ever again Elise and Rod returned home to find an invitation from the neighbour for tea.

They put on their best clothes, bought flowers and chocolates. Arrived punctually at the allotted time and found the neighbours dressed in jeans, seated round the coffee table.

When we were invited to coffee and cakes with Margarethe, a Norwegian farmer's wife, we were faced with at least five different cakes and desserts to choose from. After a half hour, which showed our hostess to be decidedly uncomfortable, we had been expected to serve ourselves. So we did so. Then we were expected to do the same with every cake on the table.

Louise is married to a Norwegian and she has now become accustomed to the custom of helping yourself. She is no longer offended when her local guests help themselves to seconds before she has finished serving herself with firsts.

Belinda is South African and married to Chris, who is British. Soon after they moved into their first home near Gatwick, Belinda invited some new friends round for a real South African braii or barbecue. Again it was to be a casual affair and, as was the custom in her homeland, Belinda invited her guests to bring their own meat as well as a bottle. This may have gone down well at our Middle East beach parties, but it did not go down well in Gatwick. The guests were affronted to be asked to provide their own food. The barbecue was not a success.

Over the years the customs we glean from our foreign friends start to rub off. Since Norway, we now toast everyone at the table with the word *skol* and look them in the eye before we drink. Elise and Rod now truly prefer real coffee. From France we have adopted the highly un-English habit of making a meal stretch to fit the number of uninvited guests who may suddenly appear as the food is served. We choose to drink jasmine tea with Chinese food and even prefer to use chopsticks.

Over time, expatriates learn to be flexible. They are happy to bring their own bottles, sausages or steaks. They merrily turn up half an hour or more after the allotted time, bring beer instead of wine, forget the flowers, open the chocolates themselves and hand them round without complaining once that they have been served instant coffee.

Jo Parfitt has lived abroad since the day after her wedding in 1987 – in Dubai, Oman, Norway and now the Netherlands. She has written a book year since she was 23 and now helps others to make writing dreams come true. She runs Summertime Publishing and Expat Bookshop.

www.joparfitt.com
www.summertimepublishing.com
www.expatbookshop.com
Blog: www.joparfitt.com
Twitter: @joparfitt @expatbooks
Facebook: www.facebook.com/summertimepublishing

Death of a Dutch Birthday Party
Niamh Ni Bhroin, Irish in The Netherlands

A Dutch birthday party faux pas

Two blueberry muffins, a chocolate éclair and just finishing off a large piece of Victoria sponge. A typical afternoon tea with my expat friends. Lynn suddenly received a text from her recently-arrived girlfriend who had been invited to her first Dutch birthday party. She had texted a message from the birthday party. All it said in the text was 'circle of death'. I promptly nearly choked on the remnants of my Victoria sponge and had a major flashback to my first initiation of the famous Dutch birthday party. It was twenty four years ago and still very fresh in my memory. We all gave each other knowing looks and felt very sorry for the newcomer. We were veterans at the party game and knew that one had to experience it first-hand. We chuckled and a plate of homemade scones was passed around.

I was three months in the Netherlands, madly in love and dying to sample the local customs. I had heard through the grapevine that nobody stands up and circulates at Dutch parties. Everybody sits in a circle and drinks coffee. I thought my expats friends' stories were slightly exaggerated, especially when the beer crates were empty at our own parties. After all, my Dutch boyfriend laughed at my jokes and it was a relief that I didn't have to explain them to him. His Dutch friends were different. Yes, they were. They seemed lively in our company.

We walked into the small living room. It was propped full with chairs all strategically placed in a very large circle. A sort of déjà vu feeling sent shivers down my spine. The narrow salon table had an array of tiny coffee cups that reminded me of my dolls' tea parties in my childhood. Blue-and-white, pink fragile forget-me-knots, painted on chipped and cracked surfaces. Three colourful ceramic bowls were filled with nuts. It seemed that we were too late for the cake. The cake and biscuits had already disappeared into the large biscuit tin that was neatly displayed on the bar counter. I had been informed of this possibility. Two fold-up garden chairs were handed to us so that we could join in the now silent company. They had no doubt heard about Lucas' new foreign girlfriend. The fish-tank stares were no exaggeration. I had been forewarned about that too. I gulped and my mouth opened and closed, gasping for air.

Lucas and my Dutch teacher had explained the protocol to me. I hadn't taken it seriously. I assumed that it was a medieval ritual!!

"You have to go around the whole room and congratulate not only the person who celebrates their birthday but everybody present. Just say 'Gefeliciteerd'. You also have to give a handshake when you say the word. Don't forget that". GE-FEL-IC-IT-EERD...

I proceeded with the formality, struggling with the now folded-out garden chair in my left hand and manoeuvring myself between the expectant blur of faces that stared at me. It didn't help that a sea of extremely long legs battled with me. I found a place miraculously and Lucas effortlessly found his own space opposite me. He gave me a nod and a roll of the eyes. It was my clue to stand up and congratulate everybody. I didn't even know at this stage who the birthday boy was. I didn't care! Small droplets of sweat started accumulating on my forehead and I started to shake the nearest hand to me. Beam me up Scottie now. Dr Spock, de-molecularize me and you needn't bother recording it in the Captain's log. Captain Kirk, I'd even snog you if you made me disappear!

My mind was blank. What was the bloody word again that went with the handshake? I couldn't remember it. I thought back to the lean Dutch teacher called Wim. My cheeks enflamed, I took a deep breath. I remembered. Oh, Thank God. There is a God.

GE-CON-DOL-EERD.

GE-CON-DOL-EERD.

I went around very quickly and said the magic words. Twenty-five handshakes later, I sat down exhausted, relieved and dying for a cup of tea. I looked up and the silence was unnerving. I gave Lucas a triumphant smile.

The birthday boy stood in front of me.

"I'm not dead. Not yet."

I had wished them all comfort in their loss. GECONDOLEERD was what you said at funerals to the grieving relatives. It was very much the opposite of congratulations.

I replied sheepishly "It all sounds double Dutch to me".

No laughter, nothing. The clock struck four on the wall opposite. The long legs shifted uncomfortably and seemed to move further away from me. A disappointed boyfriend lowered his head. No smiles there then. I found it hilarious and giggled to myself. I felt like I was in church again like a naughty teenager, trying to keep in the explosive laughter that was going to erupt at any minute. I excused myself to go to the bathroom. I just about made it and let it all out. Tears of laughter streamed down my face and echoed through the minuscule bathroom. I couldn't stop. It reached hysterical proportions. I had to pull myself together. They could hear me. But that made things even worse. I didn't care at that stage. Eventually, I pulled myself together and returned to the funeral party.

I was ignored for the rest of the afternoon. I didn't dare ask for a cup of tea! The circle of death was complete. I had even complicated things by acknowledging that it was like a funeral. I wasn't mortified. I was too depressed. I had more fun at Auntie Pam's wake when we drank copious bottles of whiskey and celebrated her life!

My boyfriend shook all the extended hands yet again before leaving.

I didn't.

Haunted by an abusive past that lasted until she met a Masai Warrior, Niamh attended a shamanic weekend in Scotland aged fifty. After leaving her marriage and transforming her life she is now the author of The Singing Warrior, *a higher self-coach and a visual mentor.*

www.thesingingwarrior.com
Blog: www.thesingingwarrior.com
Twitter: @NiamhWarrior

Deliverance
Shelley Antscherl, English in The Netherlands

Speaking a foreign language can be Double Dutch

With Blighty in the throes of gloomy recession, it seemed like the perfect time to make a new life overseas. My husband had accepted a job in a rural part of West Friesland and it felt like we were evacuating a sinking ship for the Promised Land. Our new home was a remote village in the middle of nowhere but we were looking forward to the peaceful tranquility, and anyway we had a stack of board games to keep us amused until we found some new chums to have dinner parties with.

It was sad leaving behind much-loved friends, glorious London and rolling countryside, but instead we were getting wonderful Amsterdam an hour down the road, and a cyclist's paradise of flat open countryside. Besides, we had no plans to live in Holland forever, this was a stepping-stone to our North American dream, we just had to knuckle down and throw ourselves into village life. So, it was a tad deflating on the day we arrived to see an altogether different vista to the one from the balmy summer weekend of our first reconnaissance trip.

The bright green fields dotted with pretty black and white cows under a big blue sky, had been replaced in December, by endless flat prairies of ploughed brown mud, shrouded in a freezing grey mist. The picturesque landscape we remembered now resembled a Russian steppe in winter, and after a particularly robust tornado.

We nicknamed our new home *Deliverance*, and the moniker stuck for the next 952 days. But with pioneer spirit and knowing that spring was around the corner, we looked forward to an exciting future.

However, the first few weeks ground along in a fog of exhausted befuddlement as I juggled four young children amidst a daily dose of culture shock and a peculiar sounding language that resembled nothing I'd ever heard before. Gradually though, I tuned in to the guttural noises and hacking sounds the locals used to communicate with each other and within a few weeks, I was getting the hang of this wonderfully throaty vernacular. So with courage bolstered and my trusty phrase book to hand, I set off for the local garden centre in search of a cherry tree to cheer up the front garden.

Finding an assistant, I dispensed with my usual phrase of: 'Do you speak English?' and boldly launched straight into what I wanted: '*Ik wil een Kerstboom*,' I said confidently.

"We sold out weeks ago," came the reply in Dutch, and in a tone that suggested I was a bit of a moron. No cherry trees in a big Dutch garden centre? How very bizarre I thought, and assuming he hadn't understood, I tried again:

"*Ik wil een* KERST-BOOM," I said, louder this time, and with helpful hand signals gesturing the big round cherries that would eventually hang off the branches.

But instead of pointing me in the direction of the fruit

trees, he gave me a disdainful look and brusquely told me to come back in November when there would be lots to choose from.

Disappointed, I left empty handed, bumping into someone I knew on the way home. Repeating what I'd said to the assistant, my companion grinned knowingly and started giggling as she explained that I hadn't asked for a cherry tree, which when correctly pronounced, was in fact '*kerseboom*'. Instead I'd been assertively demanding a Christmas tree – in the middle of February.

But speaking the lingo was the least of our worries, because in the meantime we had far more pressing concerns. There was absolutely nothing to do in the village, and we were gasping for a social life. Literally, *anything* to break up the tedium of yet another Saturday night Trivial Pursuit contest, between me and my equally bored husband.

A bracing bike ride in an icy gale was the favourite pastime in Deliverance, but to suburban Londoners, pedaling along the local *dijk* in the freezing cold wasn't fun, much to the consternation of our blissfully windswept and rosy-cheeked fellow villagers. And the locals we met just didn't *do* dinner parties or celebrate occasions by going out to restaurants, and besides there was nowhere to go in a 10 mile radius.

Villagers never sat down to a meal with friends unless it was something deep-fried, smothered in orange breadcrumbs and washed down with a bottle of *Amstel*. Even then they were likely to be furiously pedaling home by 6 o'clock sharp. So it was with some excitement and a sense of relief when we accepted an invitation to a neighbour's birthday party.

I booked a babysitter, planned my outfit and looked forward to a convivial evening spent engaging in witty repartee with the locals, munching on tasty hors d'oeuvres and who knows, maybe even a spot of dancing?

That night we set off for the party. Rob in a freshly pressed shirt and chinos ensemble, and me tottering perilously in killer heels and expensive designer jeans. What to take? A decent bottle of Merlot seemed appropriate. But we were in for a shock.

Arriving at the party was like turning up to a wake, only dressed as a clown. As we walked into the sitting room, other guests stopped chatting and gawped as we were ushered to a circle of chairs and sat down amongst a gaggle of serious-looking men and women across three generations, all drinking coffee. The conversation seemed to revolve entirely around what was going on in the village. Thank God for vino, I thought to myself, because I was going to need gallons that night.

But sadly there wasn't any red wine. Clearly our bottle was being squirreled away for another time as I was handed a plastic beaker of white plonk and Rob was given a beer to quaff from the bottle. Not even attempts to amuse them with my Christmas tree story could raise a chuckle and instead as I looked around at the audience, I was met with the same bemused expressions that I'd seen in the face of the garden centre assistant. Within an hour we were frantically trying to find an excuse to escape as we began fantasizing about an exciting game of Trivial Pursuit, at home.

Birthday parties were a stark introduction to rural Dutch social customs as we soon learned that strong coffee, cake and leaving promptly, formed the bedrock for any gathering in the wilds of North Holland. But ironically, as I write this from my new home in beautiful British Columbia, I can now look back on our sentence in *Deliverance* with an amused fondness that I didn't feel at the time. Because although it felt like being stuck in the Twilight Zone, endless summer picnics and family bike rides along the *dijk* were an idyllic nod to a bygone age, and much to our surprise we eventually made a handful of wonderful friends. And anyway, as Friedrich Nietzsche once said: "What doesn't kill us makes us stronger," and even if he was mistaken, I can now boast of a fine talent for useless trivia.

Shelley Antscherl is an English journalist and mother of four, now living in British Columbia, Canada. She writes for Dutchnews.nl and various publications and websites.

www.shelleyantscherl.com
Blog: blogs.bclocalnews.com/disparatehuisvrouw/
Twitter: @S_Antscherl
Facebook: www.facebook.com/pages/Disparate-Huisvrouw/216824185042258

Kissing and the Art of Keeping Friends
Jo Parfitt, English in Norway

When do we kiss, bow or shake hands?

I have to admit that when Jeanette kissed me in
church during The Peace I was rather taken aback. In our
church back in rural Rutland everyone was embarrassed
about shaking hands, let alone kissing. There they just
grudgingly offered their hands to the people in the pews
directly in front and behind and said 'Peace be with
you' as quickly as they could before lowering their eyes
and pretending to look for a tissue. Not in Stavanger,
Norway. Here they walked gaily between the rows of
grey moulded plastic chairs, shaking hands with every
single member of the congregation. Apart from Jeanette,
bless her heart. Clad in purple from her lipstick to her
opaque tights. Jeanette laid her cheeks alternately on
mine. It was as if she brushed my face with cashmere.
Silently. No puckered lips. No smackeroo. A token
gesture I suppose, for Jeanette had never set eyes on
me before. I could hardly have expected a proper kiss,
now could I? In Norway, it appears, they have perfected
the kissless kiss. All show and no feeling. Like their

mountains, so breathtakingly beautiful yet bloody cold. Yes, the Norwegian kiss is a sorry affair and their official handshake is sadly similar to the fish they sell and smoke in abundance.

Thinking of purple Jeanette led me to consider kissing in more detail. And no, I didn't dash over to embrace the vicar, instead. I contemplated the finer art of making friends and how important the greeting ritual can be.

When I left England, I was pretty reserved. A kiss for my granny at bedtime. One for my godmother. One for each parent to say thank you for a present. All on the cheek of course. Bang in the middle. Wouldn't want to touch lips, that could be classed as incest (besides, it was pretty disgusting). I had kissed my boyfriends, of course, and not usually on the cheek, but girlfriends ... uh oh, there was another dodgy area.

Not that all English people are as tight fisted with kisses, of course. Celebrities and luvvies do far too much of it. They kiss people they don't even like, calling them 'dharling' as they place cupids bows of pearly lipstick rather closer to the mouth than I would have dared.

I'd not quite mastered that sort of kiss. In fact I was so paranoid about getting it wrong when friends came to dinner, that I usually fumbled with the door handle and their coats so long that they forgot about it altogether. At least, that's what I told myself.

But then, as I said, I went abroad. At 15 in Germany, staying with my pen-friend, I learned to shake hands with everyone in the room. It was formal, polite and not too embarrassing at all. Then I studied French at university and landed up in France. There, handshaking was strictly for business and strangers.

At 21, I found myself employed as a teacher of English conversation. Before long, I was embracing my 14-year-old pupils in the High Street with ease. *Pas de problème* as they say. I kissed my friends and they kissed me, twice if they knew me and three times if they liked me a lot. I learned to kiss everyone I knew and shake hands with those I didn't when I entered a social gathering, and then to kiss them all regardless on the way out. It didn't take long to discover that what we call French kissing; they only save for their very closest friends of all.

Then I went back to England and found myself not quite knowing what to do with my lips every time I saw an old friend. Kissing wasn't quite done at Hull University.

Five years later, I married Ian, became an expat wife and went to live in the Middle East, There, I wasn't even allowed to hold hands with him in public, let alone kiss him at the airport. My own husband. But behind high walls and in lofty apartments there was a lot of kissing. Once on each cheek for anyone you came to know every time you saw them. Not in the coffee shop, or by the pool of course, but at parties and there were lots of them. Kissing meant that friends became friendlier more quickly, and with so many people moving on after a couple of years you needed to make them fast. It was either that or stay lonely.

As the years passed I became so used to kissing that I no longer fumbled with the door handle at dinner parties. There was no question that kissing was only a possibility. It happened every time. Our circle of friends grew from fellow Brits who'd do it twice to the Dutch who'd do it thrice and even to the Swiss who did it four whole times. I'd look up just before commencing the ritual, check what number they were, and go for it with gusto. It made sense to go for the highest number, particularly as I came from a country that had no official number at all. I often wondered what would happen if a French woman met a Dutch man, would he defer to her paltry two, or would she rise to meet his three?

In Norway I met a charming Argentian couple. They invited us to their home for coffee and cakes, which is what you do in Norway. No kissing happened on arrival, but it felt sort of strange, after ten previous kiss-filled years, not to kiss them goodbye to show our appreciation. Elena put up her hand as I leaned forwards at the door.

"Argentians don't really do it, you know," but she kissed me once for show.

Carlos didn't care. "I'll take two," he said with a grin and dived right in.

So what do you do if you go to England, where they don't really do it at all, and meet an English friend you used to kiss twice when you were in Dubai? Do you still kiss them, now you're home? I think you do. And what if a Norwegian meets a French person? They both do it twice, of course, but does one do it silently and the other with a smack? Or do they both kiss the air and hope the other doesn't notice?

I heard another funny story on this theme.

Rachel Leroux, as an American, is used more to hugging than kissing. Big Macs, big hats, big country and big hugs. No soppy cheek-touching for them. If they do kiss someone, it's bang on the lips. No wonder they have high self esteem.

Now Rachel married a French man called Pierre and I'm sure she is happy to do it twice, or even three times with him. But one day in Paris, she met an old American friend and they hugged. Pierre's jaw dropped a mile, convinced that the hug was a sign they were having an affair. Hugging is apparently what only lovers do in France, not friends.

The Arabs, Eskimos and butterflies rub noses. The Germans, as I said, shake hands, while the other Europeans do a lot of kissing. Meanwhile the ones, who once ran the British Empire, shuffle on the doorstep, flap their hands about a bit, look at their feet and then, if they're feeling brave, they kiss you once, right in the middle of your cheek. Only they don't know which side to aim for, and neither does their guest and so they bang noses, or glasses or both. Or worst of all, they end up kissing on the lips!

Jo Parfitt has lived abroad since the day after her wedding in 1987 – in Dubai, Oman, Norway and now the Netherlands. She has written a book year since she was 23 and now helps others to make writing dreams come true. She runs Summertime Publishing and Expat Bookshop.

www.joparfitt.com
www.summertimepublishing.com
www.expatbookshop.com
Blog: www.joparfitt.com
Twitter: @joparfitt @expatbooks
Facebook: www.facebook.com/summertimepublishing

Linguistic Gymnastics
Christine Yates, English in Germany

Language slip-ups

As adults, how do we proceed from no knowledge of a language to its full comprehension and application? There are stages. First, you have to banish any feelings of embarrassment; second, you have to listen to how the natives speak and mimic them; and third, you have to apply what you have learnt in a real situation. This sounds good in practice but can produce howlers of legendary size. Here are two, for which, unfortunately. I have become famous. My husband, David, bilingual in German, has dined out on these bloomers.

Mimicry does not always work. After long minutes of hovering around the deli counter in a supermarket, trying to think how I might ask for what I wanted and get it — a feat I had so far never accomplished — a German lady came to the counter, and, speaking clearly, asked for four slices of peppered salami and received what she wanted.

That worked, I thought, *I'll copy what she said*. So I practised a few times by the bottled gherkins then strode to the counter and announced my heart's desire, I got what I wanted too.

Unable to contain my pride, in executing alone and successfully the simplest of domestic tasks, I relayed all gloriously to a beaming husband.

"But what exactly did you say?" he asked.

Smiling exultantly I told him.

"You cannot have said that!" he said, falling backwards off his chair.

"I did, I really did," I insisted.

Pride came before a fall. David collapsed in a heap and when he had composed himself informed me that I had asked for four peppered portions of rather embarrassing slices of the female anatomy. I never returned to that shop again.

My language skills eventually improved so much that I could be gainfully employed and began working for the British Consulate in Frankfurt. There was lots of contact with rather serious and status-conscious German government officials. I soon fell into the swing of the language and rattled on at a rate of knots, my accent was good and belied the short time I had been really speaking the language. Nevertheless, now and again an English sound would pop out in the middle of a German sentence, with the most embarrassing consequences.

One day I was calling a female senior Government official within the prison service.

"Good morning, my name is Christine Yates and I'm calling from the British Consulate. It has been a little difficult reaching you this morning, so before we go any further could you tell me whether you have diarrhoea?"

I heard myself say it and frantically tried to put my tongue into rewind. The silence at the other end of the phone was ear-splitting.

I had meant to say 'direct dial extension' but pronounced an *f* instead of a *v*; fortunately, she forgave me.

Writer and editor, passionate about words and expression, creative personal development, and transitions. Ten years abroad as peripatetic execuwife; now a happily unmarried smallholder and salsa dancer.

www.journeywords.co.uk
Blog: www.journeywords.co.uk/blog.php
Twitter: @journeywords

The Fine Art of Haggling
Mark Eadie, English in Madagscar and the Sultanate of Oman

When shopping can be fun – even for a man

Mark's Guide to Haggling

- Haggle everywhere — except McDonalds and Burger King.
- If the shopkeeper is smiling; you are being over charged.
- If he calls you my friend he means exactly that.
- Walk away many times, complain that you have seen better across the road, and maybe even come back a few times over a few months.
- Beware of free offers — if you buy this, I will give you four Chinese tyres free.
- When the seller starts sweating or starts working out complicated calculations.

Consumer choice is an expectation for Europeans in particular. The luxury of being able to compare brands and models in one store needs to be left behind when one departs for the Middle East or Africa.

For many, many centuries shopping in the Arab and African world has centred on the *souk* or market. One street will have all the gold-sellers, frequently called the Street of Gold-sellers, surprisingly enough. Another will have all the spice merchants, another, the carpet-dealers, and so on. The astute shopper can quickly check out which shops have the bargains, and can jump backwards and forwards between sellers, arguing the price. This haggling, often within sight of other sellers, helps keep the price in check. If you do not like haggling, take plenty of money.

Many goods are sold by only one agent or dealer, so if you want to compare different makes you will have to go to different dealers. This was no problem in the old days when all the shops were in the souk. Now, the dealers will be spread out all over the town, and comparing an Aiwa TV with a Panasonic TV may mean a 30 minute hike through traffic to another part of town. If you have more than a couple of brands in mind, expect to spend a month getting to all the dealers. In any one showroom, you will be able to see everything made by Panasonic, from fax machines to air-conditioners, but getting to the lowest price requires you first to decide exactly what you want.

On the other hand, very basic items, or the slightly obscure, can take on grail-like searches. We once needed a jubilee clip for a garden hose. For more than six months we checked in likely shops, all over Madagascar. Not a chance. Then suddenly, in a sedate and leafy suburb we stumbled upon a small warehouse that sold virtually nothing but jubilee clips.

We spent nine months trying to find something to stop woodworm, by the time we found it, it was too late.

Sometimes, the best bargains are the ones to be avoided

most of all. For years, the cheapest tyres in Madagascar were Chinese-made and did not fit a single vehicle ever imported to the country.

But whatever you want, negotiate the price. The newcomer to 'market negotiation' is usually filled with apprehension about haggling. A New Zealander friend refuses, to this day, to haggle, explaining that she would hate to lose those smiles and handshakes whenever she goes shopping in the market. She pointed out that stall holders come out to greet her in the street and welcome her with open arms. There is a reason for this, Alison.

Recognise that you will never win at the bargaining game. This is a cultural end-game that was perfected during the Pre-Cambrian era. We managed to get a carpet down from 1700 Dirhams to 380 Dirhams over three days. The seller was almost in tears as we paid, and we felt a bit glum as we drove off. Had we exploited the poor guy? I looked in the mirror as I pulled out and saw him and his mate grinning away.

Mark and his family have lived in Africa, the Far East, Middle East and Europe, but are now back in England.

Mind Your Language
Jude Jarvis, British in the Netherlands

It's not how you say it, but what you say

One of the scariest things about moving abroad
is being confronted with a language that you understand
very little of. When I relocated to Germany, I decided
to avoid this by taking lessons before we went. I'm
not the best student, but by the time we moved I had
learned enough to read a menu and greet people. Upon
discovering that I was moving to a small town in Bavaria
my teacher taught me the word for humid, saying that
it would be useful. She was right. Within the first few
weeks it seemed like I had cause to moan about it being
too *schwjl* nearly every day. One muggy afternoon
I was sitting in a cafe with Caroline, my new German
teacher. We were sitting inside to take advantage of the
air conditioning and as he took our order the waiter
remarked on this, asking if it was too hot outside.

"*O ja, es ist viel zu schwul draußen.*"

I noticed Caroline staring at me. "What did you just say?"

"*Es ist viel zu schwul draußen*. It's too humid out. Why, what's the problem?"

It was then I learnt that when my previous teacher had taught me this new word, what she had failed to tell me was that *schwül* (humid) is an easy mispronunciation away from *schwul* (homosexual). I had just complained to the waiter that it was far too homosexual outside! I don't know how many times previously I had used the wrong word, but I never complained about the humidity again.

While in Germany I continued with my lessons. I had a few German friends that I would practice any new words or phrases on. My favourite was Christoph, a colleague of my husband, as he appreciated my attempts and corrected me without making me feel like a complete idiot. Only that morning I had learnt how to tell someone they were annoying me and, being the type who can become easily irritated, I was eager to try it out.

"Hello Jude, how are you? How is the German going? Have you learnt anything new? Do you want to try it out on me, you can always practice your German with me. So, what have you learnt that is new?" That was pure Christoph. He never used just one word when several sentences were at his disposal.

"Well I did learn something new today. Can I try it out?"

Christoph smiled and nodded.

"Okay then. Are you ready? *Du kotzt mich an!*"

The smile fell from his face. "Oh Jude, do I? I really hope not." He walked away, looking sad.

I was confused. Okay, so it wasn't the nicest thing to say, but it wasn't that bad and surely he knew I didn't mean it. I was just practicing, as he had suggested. I rushed after him to explain.

It wasn't until a few days later that I discovered "*du kotzt mich an*' roughly translates as 'you disgust me', and is one of the most insulting things you can say to a German. To reassure you: it is not always me that makes the mistake. We had been living in Germany for about a year at this point and were having dinner with some friends. The day before I had been to the hairdresser's for the first time since the move. I had deferred going for all this time as I had been worried that I would ask for the wrong thing and end up with a mullet. As it happened the appointment had gone well, and I was pleased with my new style. We were halfway through dinner when my Polish friend, Sylvia, noticed something:

"Jude, you have had your hair cut.'"

"Yes, I got it done yesterday." I patted the bottom of my bob and awaited the inevitable compliment.

"It looks," there was a pause, "quite nice."

Sitting next to her, another friend, Rob, almost spat his wine out.

"You can't say that."

"Why not. It is quite nice. It was a compliment."

"No. Saying it's very nice is a compliment." He laughed. "Saying it's 'quite' nice is like saying it isn't very nice at all."

Sylvia looked confused. I didn't blame her. *Quite* is one of those words in English that changes its meaning depending on the context. I'd understood what she meant. That was what mattered.

"I see." She looked thoughtful. "Jude, I like your haircut. It is much better than the one you had before."

Aspiring writer, terrible housewife, procrastinator extraordinaire. Currently enjoying life following her husband, as he works his way around Europe.

Facebook: www.facebook.com/jude.jarvis

Body Language Blunders
Christine Yates, English in Germany

It's not what you say, but how you say it

I had just arrived in Frankfurt and was practising regularly the only three German phrases I knew – 'Can I try it on?' 'Do you take credit cards?' 'Two beers, please' — guess what I was doing that summer! A 'single' wife (no kids and a husband absent all week), I was determined to split open the nut of overseas living, determined to prove that I could plant my acorns of independence and positive that I would enjoy, within weeks, the shade of the great oaks of success which would, undoubtedly, spring up. The naiveté of novelty! I launched myself at the city, sight-seeing at fever pitch and torturing my mouth to produce sounds which, I was reliably told, were actually words in German! Faced with a Berlin Wall of German grammar and a feeling of chipping away paint, not bricks, I dashed through life in splendid isolation, mentally shipwrecked on a foreign shore and unsure whether the natives were friendly! Long stretches of solitude compounded the teenage awkwardness and self-consciousness I felt, exactly the same at fourteen as at thirty-four. The result? A siege mentality!

Spools of unreasonable 'what if...' situations ran before my eyes. What if I did the wrong thing, said the wrong word? What if I couldn't understand what was being said to me? Worse, what if I were caught out as a foreigner? Would I be branded as an impostor and hounded down the street by crowds of cheated Germans yelling 'Fraud' after me? The dangers of a too vivid imagination and an ebb-tide of self-confidence combined to a peculiar effect.

We've all read about how animals in packs recognise they're superior and make subservient gestures to avoid appearing as a threat. Well, Pavlov's dogs had nothing on me! I began to mimic 'pack' behaviour. Not in large open spaces — there I felt no threat — but more especially in small rooms, like cafés, or confined spaces, like trains and, the worst, lifts. A marble and glass elevator, packed full of bright-jacketed German men and steel-hairdo'ed German women would inspire such 'angst' in me that my heart would race and my mouth go dry at the horror of the 'what if...' scenario! I would try, nonchalantly, to appear inconspicuous — hard when you're six feet tall in shoes, wear bright red lipstick and have a happy knack of tripping up in public! I'd smile and smile but not as a heroine in a novel would do with a gentle smile playing about her lips. My smile (more a grimace really), would gallop and cavort about my lips like it had a bit part in an amateur musical production and was about to have its five minutes of fame. No heroine's composure for me, grinning undirectionally, avoiding eye contact, tilting my head a little to one side (though I could never work out on which side to leave it) so I seemed passive and unassertive. Slouching ever so slightly (never a problem to anyone who has spent their adolescence being taller than the boys), trying desperately to absorb my height in a concertina of stomach rolls. If I'd had a tail I would have wagged it! No threat, no threat, not me, not me was *supposed* to be the message my body language proclaimed! I thought how kind it was of people to make space for me and attributed their sideways glances to nothing more than ordinary Teutonic curiosity, their unseemly haste to quit the elevator to nothing more than a laudable diligence to duty.

The day Truth dawned was the day I descended almost alone in a lift with mirrors!

Imagine how you'd react to travelling in a confined space with a rolling-headed, pop-eyed, red-lipped, grinning, sagging, bobbing women standing next to you? My fears disappeared with the opening of the doors, as, I am sure, did those of my travelling companions! How low we will let ourselves go before we will let ourselves rise! If I could look like this without words, then it was not possible to look any more ridiculous by getting a word wrong! The standard was set. The only way was UP!

Writer and editor, passionate about words and expression, creative personal development, and transitions. Ten years abroad as peripatetic execu-wife; now a happily unmarried smallholder and salsa dancer.

www.journeywords.co.uk
Blog: www.journeywords.co.uk/blog.php
Twitter: @journeywords

When's Dinner? A Confusing Concept, Even For a Native Speaker
Carrie Sanderson, Dutch-English in the UK

Who knew sharing food could be so complicated?

"What's up, Cazza?" Dave, my Business Studies course-mate, says. I've only known Dave since the start of our first year at the University of Sheffield (UK), about two months now, and he already likes to tease me with this name.

"Hi Davey-wavey! How are you?" Two can play that game. We sit down for our Marketing lecture in a newly-converted church. It's clean, modern and I can still smell the paint. We take our usual seats on the balcony, in the middle, third row back. Sleepy-eyed students slowly stream into the church.

"Yeah, fine thanks. How was hockey yesterday?" Dave asks. He takes off his dark grey jumper. It feels warm in the church today.

"Not too bad. We drew, but we were losing, so not a bad result," I reply, getting my blue ball-point pen and notepad ready. It is still a few minutes before the plump, bald American professor would start the lecture and no doubt tell us all about the wonderful Wonderbra brand; funny how every single lecture he seems to reference it. Could he ever talk about anything else? Dave mentioned once that we should have a sweepstake; guess how long it takes before Professor Kottler mentions Wonderbra? Not a bad way to make some extra cash.

"Have you started the Marketing essay yet?" I ask Dave.

"Sort of. Written a few rough notes. Hey, do you want to come over tomorrow to go through it together and I'll cook dinner?"

"Cool, yeah that would be helpful," I say, thinking that might kick-start my assignment. I am still finding it hard to write essays in English since leaving my Dutch school back in June. Even though I spoke English at home with my British parents, all my school work was done in Dutch. Of course the English lessons were done in, you guessed it, English. But it's not the same as having *all* your lessons in English and writing *all* your work in English.

The next morning I catch up with Dave at our Economics lecture.

"So, what time do you want me to come over for dinner?" I ask.

Dave scrunches up his face and doesn't know whether to laugh or not.

"What's wrong?" I say with a confused look on my face. Did I ask a stupid question? I don't think I did. I rack my brain to find an answer, but I can't come up with one. Surely asking someone what time they want you over for dinner is a simple yet useful question? I didn't want to turn up at the wrong time. If I was too late, the food would be burnt. If I was too early, well, my tummy would be growling at me for getting it wrong and having to   wait to be fed.

"At *dinner* time, Cazza," Dave says. "When did you think?" He laughs at me.

"But what time, Dave?" I press again. "6pm? Or 7pm?"

"Wait a minute! You were thinking it was tonight?" Dave says.

"Yes, tonight. Dinner-time is in the evening, isn't it? And you said you'd cook dinner." I feel heat rising up from my neck and into my cheeks. Dave is almost on the floor. If we weren't in a public place and he wasn't wearing his favourite jeans, he probably would have been rolling around clutching his stomach.

"Dinner-time is around noon for me, you're talking about tea-time," Dave says. "Cazza, I'm from the North where it's dinner and tea. People from the South say lunch and dinner, *dharling*!"

The penny drops. I'd heard before that fellow Brits interchangeably use the words 'lunch' and 'dinner' for the same thing, but I'd never got confused by it. My family had always used 'lunch' for lunch and 'dinner' for dinner. They never used dinner to mean lunch, or so I remembered. Or had they? And to make it more complicated some folk use the word 'tea' to mean 'dinner'... how was I ever going to learn what people meant?

"So you were going to turn up tonight, were you?" Dave smiles. He still thinks the situation is hilarious.

"Yes, that's what I mean by dinner," I try to explain. "I didn't know you used the word dinner for lunch!" I am bright red. I want to sink into the ground and disappear.

I can't believe that even though I am English I did not know about these differences. I'd always thought tea-time was having a cup of tea and a piece of cake. Born and brought up in The Netherlands and having visited England on many occasions during my childhood, I can't believe now is the time I get caught out. And in front of Dave whom I know will never let me live this down. From now on, I'll have to question everyone who says 'dinner' to find out which meal they mean. What if I was meeting someone for a date? I wouldn't want to get that wrong!

There and then it dawns on me that even though my passport states I am British, I still have a lot to learn about being British. Who would have known? Maybe I am more Dutch than I'd realised. Now there's a thought.

Carrie Sanderson is a writer and the owner of Health & Healing, UK. She was born and brought up in The Netherlands by English parents.

http://www.health-healing.co.uk
Blog: www.carriesanderson.com)
Twitter: @carriesanderson
Facebook: www.facebook.com/pages/Health-Healing/160616755145

Chicken
Sareen McLay, Scottish in Borneo

Playing chicken in the supermarket

Free meal vouchers, great. *Let's use them,* I thought as we were handed the vouchers on our arrival in the small town of Miri, Borneo.

The vouchers were for the local Shell club, nicknamed 'The Boat Club'. On our first evening we left the cool air-conditioned sanctuary of our sparsely furnished temporary house and headed off in the car to the club.

"I don't want to go, Mummy," Laura had groaned. Only four years old, she was our eldest daughter and she was tired and grumpy.

"Come on love, there's a super playground at the club. We can go and find it while Daddy orders us some dinner," I had tried to smile and cheer her up although inside I knew exactly what she meant. I too felt like closing the door of the house and staying there. It had been a long journey for all of us from the UK to Borneo and we were exhausted from our transcontinental move.

"I've ordered Thai noodles, chicken in black bean sauce and some French fries too, just in case." My husband

Kevin looked pleased with himself as he fetched us later on from the fabulous wooden playground.

It was not a successful dinner. With the jet lag it was really eleven o'clock in the morning for us all. The last thing the girls wanted to do was sit down and eat a big dinner. I looked at them in despair.

"Well, at least eat some French fries girls. You'll be hungry later if you don't." I tried to eat my own dinner, more from necessity than a desire to eat. I knew we would be up during the night and felt I needed all the strength I could get.

After three nights in a row of the girls picking at their dinner in the club, I decided to take control. So, on Saturday afternoon I braved the heat and headed to our local supermarket. With some trepidation I started the engine of our rental car, a Proton Waja, and drove off slowly. I had never driven an automatic before.

To leave the housing compound I had to drive over a rickety one-way bridge. The water below was brown, murky and fast flowing. I had heard that there were crocodiles in there. Nervously, I waited as the red light shone for what seemed like an eternity. Finally, the light turned to green and I cautiously edged out on to the old bridge. The wooden slabs clattered loudly underneath.

"Thank God for that," with a sigh of relief I made it to the other side and turned left into the supermarket car park. As I switched off the engine I sat for a moment in the heat. Part one done.

Known to everyone as The Pottery, the supermarket was attached to the side of a factory producing big clay garden pots. I didn't know where to begin as I walked through the sliding glass doors. The shop seemed enormous. It was dark, dusty and on closer inspection, not too clean. In some ways it reminded me of an old haberdashery shop where you could buy everything from toothpaste to paint. I wandered up and down the narrow aisles with increasing dismay. The shopping list in my hand seemed to mock me. What chance was there that I would get everything I had set out for?

The dirty, rusty trolley, I pushed along had a wobbly wheel and I wondered if I would ever be brave enough to put my children in one of them.

Finally, I located the 'Western Aisle' with its pitiful array of McVities digestive biscuits and bottles of HP brown sauce. I stood there not knowing whether to laugh or cry and oh, how I wished at that moment to be in Sainsbury's, Tesco or even Asda. Standing in the middle of that bustling supermarket with shoppers busy all around me, I had never felt so alone or lost. What was I going to do?

Turning away I walked along the rows of enormous sacks of rice, past freezers filled with bags of what looked like pigs' trotters and shelves and shelves of biscuits with strange names. Eventually, I reached the cooler cabinets and at last caught sight of something familiar. A whole chicken! There it was, sitting on a lovely polystyrene tray and wrapped in cling film. With relief I put it into my nearly empty trolley and felt my spirits lift a little.

"Roast chicken for tea, a nice easy meal," I thought to myself and headed towards the cash desk. The Malaysian Ringgits in my purse looked old and well-worn as I paid. Cash was still king here.

Buoyed up by the thought of a good plain dinner for everyone, I pushed open the door of our new home, hands full of little plastic bags from the supermarket.

"Hello. I'm back. Who would like roast chicken for tea?" I called.

"Me! Me!" two small faces look at me in delight. Pretty as little fairies, the girls were fluttering about dressed up as princesses. Kevin smiled at me in relief. I knew I looked happier again.

The gas oven was new to me and took a while to figure out. Eventually I managed to light it using a long taper and jumping back quickly from the whoosh of flames.

Out of the white plastic bag I pulled the Holy Grail, a whole chicken. As I took the cling film off, I noticed that the chicken looked ever so slightly grey. I lifted it up.

Suddenly a wrinkled old head and two scrawny legs with long yellow claws flopped down. With a gasp I dropped the thing in disgust. The cold beady eye of the chicken seemed to watch me as I turned in horror towards Kevin.

Close to tears I wondered, *what now*?

Together we searched the poorly equipped kitchen for something sharp to chop the offending appendages off. Nothing was sharp enough.

To my everlasting shame, I have to confess, we threw the chicken in the bin and went to the club once more for dinner.

Sareen left Scotland ten years ago. She lived in Oman and then Malaysia before moving to Holland in 2008 with her husband and three children.

The Durian Wars
Maria Foley, Canadian in Singapore

Local delicacies are not always what they seem

"Stop being such a baby," I scolded myself as I peered nervously into the local supermarket. The stories couldn't possibly be true, could they? A fruit that smelled worse than wet dog, unwashed jockstrap, and rotten eggs combined? It was probably just a silly tale cooked up to terrify gullible newbie expats like me. Except that each time the glass doors swooshed open to disgorge shoppers into the unrelenting Singaporean heat, I caught a whiff of something that made my insides wobble.

How bad can this durian stuff be? I wondered as I crept into the store. The answer came swiftly, enveloped in a toxic cloud of stinkyness. Actually, *stink* isn't the right word; that's far too innocuous. *Reek* doesn't quite measure up either. Even *stench* fails to fully convey the gag-inducing miasma of foulness that wafted up from the supermarket produce section. It was the kind of full-body sensory experience that hits you first in the back of the throat, curdling your uvula before continuing its path of destruction throughout your body until every cell begs for mercy.

I considered making a run for it. But then a little voice inside my head said, "Maria, you're in a strange land. Embrace difference! Be adventurous! Try..." At that point, the little voice was overcome by the noxious fumes and passed out. The point, however, had been made.

Holding my breath, I ventured closer. It wasn't hard to figure out where the durian was: I could practically see wiggly cartoon stink lines rising from the table. It even *looked* dangerous, its hard, spiky skin announcing to the world that this was a fruit to be reckoned with. This fruit, it was clear, was bad to the bone.

The concept of Fate is woven into the fabric of life in the East. Although we in the Western world tend not to embrace it to the same degree, I felt the inexorable pull of the durian and knew it was Fate that brought us to Singapore so we could conquer this most worthy of adversaries... or die trying. I bought the smallest piece I could find — Fate is all well and good, but there's no need to go overboard.

An hour later my daughters came home, and stopped dead inside the front door. "What's that smell?" they whined, wrinkling their noses.

"It's durian. We said we'd try it, remember?"

"Does it hafta be today?" Erin looked faint. "I had a really big lunch, and I won't be hungry again till breakfast."

"And I have a tummy-ache," Megan piped up, although she'd just spent the last two hours splashing and shrieking in the pool without any sign of gastrointestinal distress.

"Tomorrow, then," I said quickly. No point in pushing.

We spent an uncomfortable night. Like heat, odour

rises, and the fetid smell of durian soon permeated every room in the house. The next morning, Michael returned from a business trip. "Oh my god," he said, backing quickly out of the house. "What's that smell?"

"It's durian," I said, breathing through my mouth.

"Is it supposed to smell like that?"

"I think it's gone bad," Megan offered. "Maybe we should throw it away and get some cookies instead."

"No." I'd started this, and I was determined to see it through to the bitter end. "We're trying it. Now."

Like condemned prisoners at their final meal, we assembled in the dining room. "Who's going first?" I asked brightly. We all turned to look at Michael, the man whose cast-iron stomach has kept him from losing face (or lunch) at countless corporate banquets around the globe.

He nonchalantly popped a bit of the creamy flesh into his mouth. Three seconds later he made a funny squeaking sound, jumped up and ran to the kitchen. The *splat* of the durian forcefully hitting the sink reverberated throughout the house. The girls and I smiled uneasily at each other throughout the retching, the stream of agonized *omigods*, and finally, the unmistakable sound of a beer being opened and downed in one long swallow.

"That," he said as he staggered back into the dining room, "was revolting."

Megan valiantly offered herself up next. Her tiny piece of durian had barely touched her tongue before being spit clear across the room. It landed in a pot of orchids, which promptly wilted.

Faced with such widespread carnage, I begged Erin to put an end to the madness. "Save yourself," I pleaded, close to tears.

"We said we'd try new things," she said bravely.

"Erin, don't do it," said Megan in a strangled voice, her head between her knees. "It's really, really bad."

The spoon trembled in Erin's hand as she brought it up to her mouth. I closed my eyes and waited for the worst... but nothing happened. Opening one eye, I saw her face, scrunched up in concentration as she chewed. Finally she arrived at her decision. "It's yucky," she said, putting her spoon down and pushing the plate away.

We stared at her, stunned. "Yucky?" Michael said. "That's the worst you can say about it? *Yucky*?" She shrugged and started playing her Game Boy. As far as she was concerned, the experiment was over.

By now the fumes were making our eyes water. I couldn't delay any longer, so I did it: I ate durian.

The earth didn't heave, and neither did my stomach. In fact, it was disappointingly anticlimactic. It tasted like scallion pudding: definitely yucky, but not nearly as bad as it should have been. I had a fleeting sense of disappointment that this legendary opponent had been so easily vanquished.

Relieved to have won the durian war, we scraped the remains into the garbage can outside. But the durian had its revenge after all. Later that evening, I noticed a group of neighbours clustered together on the deck, muttering ominously and glancing over at our house.

"Good lord," I heard. "What's that awful *smell*?"

After four rocky years, Maria is now 90% adjusted to post-expatriate life. She ~~whines~~ blogs about how much she misses her expat days.

www.iwasanexpatwife.com
Twitter: @iwasanexpatwife

Travelling with Children
Karine Quillien, French in Gabon

Children, airplanes and medication do not mix

How can you spot an expatriate family? The answer, while, being a bit of a joke, is also the smallest common denominator: the KLM blue Old Dutch porcelain houses on their windowsill; not just a few examples gleaned during business trips, but the entire collection, enriched trip by trip on the many long-haul flights the migrants take back to their base country for the summer months. Those with difficult postings have emptied many of their famous alcohol: Jenever.

In 1997, we lived in Gabon, Western Africa, in an environmental paradise, totally isolated and surrounded by primary forest and jungle. I had a busy husband who could only take three weeks holiday in a row, two young children of five and eight, Lorraine and Kevin, who thought the residential camp in which we lived was 'so-ooo' boring when friends were gone during summer holiday, and a cute cat who had to be monitored even more closely than the kids. For once, we had decided it made sense for me to go back to Brittany, in France, for two months, to make sure the two little monsters remembered their roots, their cousins and their grandparents. But maybe more importantly, it was meant to raise their awareness of the 'normal' European life to which we were supposed to return at the end of the year. I needed to show them that, unfortunately, children were not allowed to go to school in shorts and T-shirts all year round, or walk barefoot in the streets. I knew I would have to crush part of the innocence legitimised by such an amazingly free lifestyle. They needed to learn that danger could lurk round every corner from both cars and adults rather than from black mambas (the venomous jungle snake) or elephants. Plume, the cat, was a fluffy cross between a fur coat and a Persian, sold to me by a European vet, who was making a fortune taking care of all the expats' pets. The vet had become a good friend and was always happy to vaccinate children or cat when required. This year, Plume was part of the long summer migration.

We had packed the suitcases with local art and crafts for the family; some needed sweaters, and the dreaded shoes. In those days, small animals were allowed in the cabin without anything more than a valid rabies vaccination. I had slightly sedated the fluffy beast to avoid any distressed meowing. My husband was genuinely dreading the quiet and empty house until he would join us a month later, but the sight of the freezer filled with his favourite dishes brought a smile back to his face. Everything was under control, my control. Furthermore, Linda, one of my friends, was also travelling the same afternoon with her two boys only a few years older than my children, so we promised to look out for each other. And my travel pills were ready. I may have forgotten to mention I get travel sick, always, whether by air, car, boat or train, to the painful point that my brain goes into 'pause' mode and spends the entire trip convincing my stomach to hold on. I am lucky enough never to be seriously ill, so the smallest amount of medication I take for any real pain has a major effect on me. The GP had prescribed three little white pills to be taken precisely five hours before departure for a maximum effect. I pulled such a wry face at the bitter taste of the medication that the children laughed and said Plume was a much better patient than Maman. But I had totally overlooked the fact that we didn't have a direct flight and that we had to wait four hours in Libreville for an international connection to Paris.

The first leg of the journey was a short flight over beautiful, unscarred jungle. The persistent green top of the canopy looked like a tapestry of broccoli heads pressed against each other. This repetitive vision and the first effects of the pills made my eyelids grow heavier. It was chaos in the international airport, packed on this first day of the summer vacation. I still remember the long queues at the departure desks, the small white children asleep on the suitcases and the African babies safely tucked in the colourful 'boubous' on the back of their mothers. I was carrying Lorraine in my arms, an emergency backpack for the night flight and the cat, while Kevin was trotting behind us, carefully watched over by my friend, Linda. In the distance I spotted the vet who happened to be on the same journey. The three of us decided to sit together. By then, two hours before our flight, I was already feeling drowsy, terribly sweaty and tired. By the end of the wait, the pills were working full blast; I couldn't hold a conversation and could barely keep my eyes open. In normal circumstances, there is nothing sexy about travelling with a summer camp and a menagerie, but this time I was blissfully unaware of my surroundings. I don't know how I went through security.

Today, I would have been arrested as some kind of junkie. I have no recollection of sitting in the plane. The full story was later given to me by my friends, concerned at first by my total lack of reaction. They decided to take matters into their own hands, asked to be seated next to us and tucked me under a blanket. Together, they shared the burden of caring for us. Linda looked after the children, made sure they ate, slept, were not cold and not frightened to see their unfit mother happily dreaming away during the entire journey, while the vet kept an eye on the cat. The flight was perfect — for me at any rate. I literally woke up in Paris, fully rested, relieved but shameful and was handed back kids and pet with a word of warning:

"Next year, please tell us which flight you are taking so we can be sure to take the next one!"

I swore never to take another sickness pill again as there is nothing worse than letting your children down and losing total control over your life. Instead, when I got back to Gabon after the summer I invited my Good Samaritan friends round for a thank you drink, so we could crack open a few more of those little Dutch houses.

From buzzing London to peaceful The Hague, via the coastline of West Africa and the tropical forests of Malaysia, Karine has lived 25 beautiful years of expatriation.

The Expat Husband
Susan Ventris, English in Norway

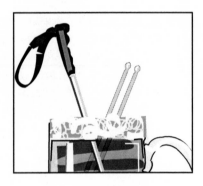

When your husband is no longer the man you married

Back home, my husband was a pretty ordinary kind of chap. During the week, he worked at the office, and watched television in the evenings. At weekends, he searched B&Q for paint stripper and applied weed killer to the garden. His idea of excitement was a trip to Homebase to look for a patio set. The most challenging thing that ever happened to him was when the DIY shop ran out of cornflower blue emulsion. You always knew where he was, in those days.

And then we were posted overseas.

Suddenly, we found ourselves living in a rented house where all our needs were taken care of. If anything went wrong around the house, we made a phone call. Nature abhors a vacuum, and so did my husband. All that pent-up energy that used to be channeled into decorating had to be used up somehow. Like many male expatriates he channeled it into sport. Rumour has it that there are men who channel their energy elsewhere. They are material for another article no doubt, but I'm not going to be the one to write it.

Not just any sport, of course. A gentle putt putt around a tennis court does nothing for the male ego. Men are naturally drawn to unusual and dangerous sports, and, by a quirk of nature, the more out of condition they are, the more death-defying the sport they tend to choose. And living abroad opens up a whole new field of sporting endeavors for the newly liberated husband. I've known husbands who've taken up bungy-jumping, and husbands who've gone off white-water rafting. Fortunately, I haven't been married to them. My husband chose skiing, a sport that was entirely new to him

Now I have nothing against skiing. It's a fine sport. My husband assured me that he was in the peak of athletic condition, and who was I to argue? I knew that he was flexible because I'd witnessed the contortions he got into painting the hall ceiling. All those sprints across the living-room to fetch the remote control for the television must have built up stamina, and everyone knows that beer is a fine body-building material. Nevertheless, I decided to err on the side of caution and took myself off to England, rather than be witness to his maiden voyage on skis.

It would not be an exaggeration to say that he sank before leaving the harbour. The exertion of putting on his ski-boots proved a little too taxing. Bending down, he experienced a sharp spasm in his back. Not wishing to appear weak in front of his Norwegian friends, all of whom had been skiing since they were in romper suits, he gamely skiied tor the rest of the day. Nature finally caught up with him when the party stopped at a café on the way home. Rising out of his chair, he experienced a further spasm as his back locked. Emitting an anguished cry of pain and humiliation, he sank to his knees. A small crowd gathered around him. In a spectacle that witnesses have described as profoundly moving, yet faintly hilarious, he was carried out to the car and driven home.

Back home his condition worsened. He crawled to the phone to request the aid of our nearest (male) neighbour. His friend cooked tea for our daughter and summoned medical assistance. The doctor arrived to discover my husband laid out on the floor complaining of back pain while his friend shuffled around the kitchen in a pinny. This is the sort of behaviour that tends to get you a reputation in a small town. I can't help thinking that none of this would have happened if we'd stayed at home.

And then there are the financial problems. Back home, our major financial decision was whether to pay the gas bill promptly, or wait until they got really nasty. A decision my husband was quite happy to leave to me. Suddenly, he found himself earning a salary the size of the national debt of a small country. For the first time, he got interested in money.

Nowadays, our home is visited regularly by the sort of people you'd normally cross the street to avoid: Insurance salesmen, financial advisors. They slap him on the back and call him by his first name. They know more about us than our mothers do, and what's more, it's all down in writing. Forms; we've filled out hundreds of them. Forms for policies we're not even interested in; forms for schemes we haven't a hope of understanding - even if we devote the rest of our lives to studying financial matters.

Not that I'm complaining. At least if something goes wrong you have someone to sue if you take financial advice. It was when my husband decided to play the stock market that things got really worrying. Expatriate men like to do that. It gives them something to talk about when they can't get about because of their injuries. He has it fifty percent right anyway. He knows exactly how to buy shares. He's a dab hand at buying. It's just the how and when to sell that seems to be causing problems.

Expatriate husbands are a funny breed. They're in the unique position of being able to fulfill their boyhood ambitions. This may not be a popular theory with the male sex, but it's arguable that most young men have fairly straightforward ambitions. They want to drive powerful cars, play loud musical instruments and travel to wacky places to perform improbably athletic feats. (There may be a few who long to devote their lives to spiritual development or services to mankind, but I've never met any). Mercifully, most men are restricted by financial obligations from fulfilling their boyhood dreams. They settle down to domesticity, where their daily habits are as predictable as the phases of the moon, and about as exciting.

Not the expatriate man, however. Given a hefty salary and undreamt of opportunities to travel, the expatriate is in a position to drink long and deep from the well of life, though some prefer to do so from a whisky bottle. Overseas, you become aware of new aspects of your husband's personality, not all of which belong to the man you married.

Even the summer holidays are a dangerous time. A time when many wives take the children back to visit their mother, rather than his. A time when husbands are never able to extend their holiday that little bit further. They wave goodbye so sadly at the departure gate and you tell them to take care. But the moment they're home alone it's a different story. Somehow they never find the time to hoover the carpet or water the plants. Neither do they summon up the energy to defrost and reheat all those carefully prepared meals for one that you laboured over in the last weeks of the school term. Instead, they feast on fast food and only telephone at three in the morning to tell you about a particularly wild evening with the boys.

One friend of mine told of the queues of wife-free expatriate husbands in the doctor's surgery, all waiting to have their earplugs removed. When the wife's away the boys really start to play.

The real trouble begins when they expect you to join them in their pursuits. I should know. I'm the sort of quiet soul who likes nothing better than to spend the evening reading Jane Austen. I like to play soothing classical music on the piano. Then my husband got his drum kit — an event he could never have hoped for in our semi back home. Loud and drunken mates appeared in our basement, equipped with electric guitars and amplifiers. I found myself mysteriously propelled towards a keyboard and instructed to just 'play a few chords'. That was four years ago and I'm still playing the same chords.

Susan Ventris is British and now lives in Perth, Australia, where she works as a naturopath.

www.susanventris.com.au

My Friend Godzilla
Phyllis Adler, American in England

When your husband turns into an animal

The door opens, the sound of a suitcase thuds to the floor... your life is about to change: your partner is returning from a business trip.

Usually, it is my husband who has been away and I have been at home with the children. While he has been gone, the tone of the house has altered. I operated with less structure and on a more equal basis with my teenage children, there was debate and we aimed for democratic decision. Calm has reigned.

Then in waltzes Godzilla!

Like any wary animal, Godzilla immediately senses the change in the atmosphere of his cave. He sniffs the air and looks about him. Godzilla reacts quickly to uneasy feelings of displacement. In order to re-establish his place by the hearth, he closely questions everyone on the issues of the week. We had all been quite proud of the methods we had used to head off our crises, but no, we soon discover how remiss we have been. Various inadequacies are pointed out plainly and bluntly. We are made to feel like failures in self-management. And if anyone knows about management, it is Godzilla. After all he has been on a business trip to another country, battled with natives and survived unscathed; while we have merely had to deal with leaky taps and un-programmable video recorders.

This is not exactly the welcome home by candle-light I envisioned during his absence. After five minutes of scrutiny. I wonder who it is exactly that I thought I was missing.

What is happening is not dissimilar to the territorial impulses we see acted out before us every day on CNN. It is simply a microcosmic example combined with the stress from the trip. Add to that the God-like symptoms that develop in those on the company expense account. This person, who has been feeling super-human in some ways, and — hopefully — a bit lonely in others, enters his lair. He is eager to become part of the whole again. But unfortunately, he has not had time to set aside the 'work-week' mode of operation and re-adjust to kitchen customs.

In my own home, this process of mini culture-shock and territoriality plays itself out in a fairly traditional setting. Currently, I do not have an office outside the home. But what if there are two of you regularly coming and going and frequently re-establishing and re-asserting territorial needs? The effects can be very hazardous, both to your marriage and your health.

When we were younger, the re-entry time for my travelling hubby was much longer than it is now. Sometimes, these days, it is down to nine not-so-easy-to-live-with minutes. At least, as with all things that you have experienced before, you develop a sure knowledge that it will pass. In the beginning of our life together, I didn't have the distance or the goodwill to realise that in large measures, with this person, it was mostly a need to be in the heart of the family again that prompted this carnage. And it took many well-chosen moments to gently let my buddy know this re-entry behaviour was not going to fly, even though he did.

Twenty six years on, we are still ironing out the kinks.

I have found comfort in knowing that this scene is not unique. Unfortunately, travelling marriages do not always reflect us at our best. Every time a plane lands, someone, somewhere will behave in this totally normal, if not enjoyable, manner. In the home, as on CNN, we are more primitive than we like to admit. Just ask my friend, Godzilla!

Printed with permission of Godzilla.
Reprinted with permission of Dual Career Network magazine.

Phyllis Adler, lawyer, mediator, and psychotherapist considers her major accomplishment was twice moving internationally with three children and a 95 pound dog, without totally losing her humour.

Finding my Ski Legs
Linda March, English in Norway

Yes, you can be too old to learn

I come from a sheltered seaside resort on the south coast of England. We get snow on average once every seven years. Ten-year-old children are beside themselves with excitement because they have never made a snowman before. Cars glide into each other at 5 mph and are abandoned because we have no winter driving skills. Residents prepare for a siege — bread and milk cannot be had for love or money. Factories, offices and schools stand empty. The snow brings us to a standstill. It's about two inches deep and lasts for one day. In other words, if God had meant me to ski he would have left me under an alpine gooseberry bush.

And if things had gone according to plan, ski slopes and I would never have bumped into each other. But, as we all know, the best laid plans of mice and, particularly men, go oft astray and so my husband, John, arrived home with the news that we were being relocated to Norway. Until that point, 'ski' had meant nothing more to me than a harmless low-fat yoghurt. How cruelly innocence is dashed. Suddenly the word seemed to be on everyone's lips and no longer with a comforting black cherry flavour, but with menacing connotations:

"Norway, how wonderful!   Fjords, snow covered mountains — you'll be able to ski."

"Who? Me? You're joking!"

"No, honestly, you'll love it. It's wonderful for the children to learn so young."

Now, I'm quite prepared to accept that otherwise sane and reasonable friends of mine, choose to mortgage themselves up to the hilt for the privilege of looking like the Michelin man, in vivid pink snowsuits, one week a year in the mountains of Italy and France. I've admired their salopettes; I've sympathised with cracked ribs and broken ankles. I don't laugh at that funny little suntan that stops at the chin. Live and let live is my motto, just don't expect me to join in.

My adamance that I am a born and bred seaside holiday-maker, and not a ski slope holiday-maker, held out for almost four months after our move, until it became apparent that in Norway skiing has nothing to do with holidays. It is an everyday occurrence and everyone does it — everyone except me, that is; everyone except me and my children. And here, of course, was the rub. Once peer pressure kicks in you've had it.

"Please can we go skiing Mummy, please, please?"

And that niggling voice of guilt... "It's wonderful for the children to learn so young."

Add to all this, the half-term arrival of John's sister, her husband and two boys and I was outnumbered seven to one.

Fortunately, the snow plough had been out on the mountain road and in the car park where we parked between house-high mounds of snow. We trudged what seemed miles in the bitter cold to the bottom at the ski lift and the little wooden hut where you could hire equipment. I pondered the advantages of the transformation from Dr Jekyll to Mr Michelin — at least you would be warm and, more importantly, you would look and feel the part. It's hard to feel like a skier in two pairs of track suit trousers, a crocheted beret and a pair of Debenhams woolly mitts. Svelte salopettes and snowsuits glided past us. I had an ominous feeling that I didn't belong here.

The first problem was getting into the hut, since we had to dodge the constantly passing ski-lifts to do so. It was rather like playing chicken on the M25. By the time I'd made it there, been fitted with horrendously stiff boots, which hurt to be stationary in and goose stepped out of the hut to make the return crossing, I had the added burden of surprisingly long and heavy skis. I had participated in enough daredevil activity for one day. I was ready for the après-ski, but the slopes beckoned.

Both John and Martin had skied 22 years before, so they were the self-appointed instructors. Unfortunately, my mental picture of a ski instructor is taller, blonder and more bronzed than John or Martin, but beggars can't be choosers. Of course, ski equipment has advanced during the past 22 years as much as John and Martin's physical prowess has declined, so it was rather like the blind leading the blind — not a comforting image when you're talking about skiing down mountain slopes. They gave us a quick demonstration of how to stop by turning your feet inwards and so 'snow-ploughing' to a halt, and then busied themselves helping the children, leaving Sue and I to fend for ourselves.

I remembered the instructions and got on my skis easily. I had a momentary thought of the whole thing being a doddle, before registering that I was on a slope and shooting off at a hundred miles an hour, screaming for help and turning my feet inwards with absolutely no result, straight into a tree. Surprisingly, I didn't hurt myself, the thick snow making a comfortable landing point, but I couldn't get up. The skis were ridiculously long and wouldn't bend in the middle, so I couldn't get my feet flat on the ground. Finally, undoing the skis, I scrambled to my feet, determined to try again. But when I looked around the realisation dawned that everywhere was on a slope and there was no escape from shooting off every time I got my skis on. I bravely had two more tries but it was like riding a bike downhill without any brakes — not much fun beyond the age of about 13. John finally tried teaching me to turn round. But after one 90 degree turn I was pointing downhill, my knuckles white from clutching the sticks so tightly, in the awful realisation that these two puny poles were the only things preventing me from hurtling off like an out of control human snowball. The only option seemed to be to have hysterics and scream at John to take my skis off. Completely disgusted, he obliged and glided off, 22 years sickeningly falling away as it all came back to him.

I can't help feeling rather ashamed in light of how well the others did. Of course, the children took to it like ducks to water and John even took the ski-lift to the top of the mountain before the day was over. We were rather surprised when we recognised people coming down for a second time, since John had disappeared to the top, but having dusted off the insurance policies it was rather like holding a lottery ticket on a Saturday night waiting for him to appear. Still, you can't win them all. He finally hove into view and slid gracefully into the dying swan position as we all cheered.

Ever optimistic, John thinks cross-country skiing may be more up my street, so perhaps one day I'll try again on a flat piece of ground. Maybe if I got used to walking about, turning and stopping, I would enjoy it. On the slope I had no control. As soon as the skis were on, I was off, if you see what I mean.

They were all addicted and two days later John took our older daughter, Milly, again. He says she's coming on in leaps and bounds — well maybe it's early days for leaps and bounds, but she's getting there. Little Elsa and I snuggled on the comfy settee, ate the packet of English biscuits Martin had brought us, and watched a video of *The Snowman* — the way God intended us to enjoy snow.

When not helping others make an impact with their written words through her proofreading and editing work, Linda is working on a novel and family history.

www.goodenglishcompany.com

Wife at Large in Paris
Louise Rankin, English in Norway

The truth about tagging along on a free business trip

"Is this your first time?" said a pink-suited lady dripping with the latest home-party jewellery.

Now I wonder how she guessed. Was it my clothes? Was it my attention to the host's words? Or were the traces of insecurity stamped all over my forehead?

Actually, I consider myself quite a seasoned traveler, but yes, this was my first trip as a business man's wife and the five other ladies in the party were all in the process of sizing each other up.

"Par for the course," I was told by a dear friend prior to departure, "but you'll love them all by the end of it." I had the gravest of doubts about the pink-suited version, but I tried to be open-minded at this early stage of the trip.

There we all were sitting round the breakfast table on the first morning. Several of the others had settled into eating the right sort of breakfast. There are certainly a few rules in this situation. You must never touch the bacon and eggs, for example, otherwise you will be labeled as a glutton. However, when you visibly look as if you already are a glutton, you must make a choice between confirming their opinion that this is why you got this fat in the first place, or go for the safe option by filling your plate with unfilling fruit and gain a few brownie points, while they commend you for making an effort.

"Have you decided what to do today?" said a Laura Ashley dressed woman with a country-fresh face.

At that moment my own cotton frock was hanging in the bathroom trying to de-crump from its journey in the smallest suitcase I have ever been known to use. I was actually inordinately proud of the fact that I could boast to my husband that he was travelling with a lady who could, this time, pack in a smaller suitcase than his own.

I had planned to take back home the odd memento, even if he had to pack it in his suitcase, but I had a funny feeling that Per had other plans. He remembers well that irresistible Portuguese pottery breakfastware set I forced him to carry on as hand luggage. It nearly made a hole in the floor of the plane back from Lisbon, as well as a hole in his pocket when he had to buy an extra holdall. I am sure it was the cause of the hostess asking some of the passengers to move to the back of the plane to balance it out.

Let's move on to the second morning breakfast. Having been shamed out of my leggings and comfy tee shirt into my crumpled frock, I was horrified to discover that Day One had obviously been the day to impress people in smart clothes. Day Two was shorts and T-shirts day.

"Oh well, at least she's trying," I could swear I heard someone muttering in the hotel corridor.

Of the five wives, I was relieved to see that there were at least two who looked as if they might be sufferable, even if one was well into her forties and was trying to be a punk model all in black, with an orange stripe in her hair. Now there were only five of us, but as soon as we went shopping it was quite clear that our differences went further than our dress size: Hooray Heidi was into classical cut glass; Punky Anne-Marie favoured spiky jewellery; Earthy Els wanted to look at recycled paper products. Sadly, the Rue St Honoré was not able to serve us all.

So we moved on to the day's cultural event. Be warned: there is always one wife who tries to take over. When we gave Heidi an inch she took a mile (a Norwegian mile at that). Literally. We spent half an hour walking round all four walls of the courtyard building of the Louvre, retracing our steps twice, only to find that the way in was where we had started. Of course we had all known that in the beginning, but no one had dared to say.

Worse was to come, because the others soon saw fit to promote me as their leader; all because I foolishly admitted to having 'O' Level French!

"I think we deserve a break," braved our pet punk, after one hour's trek through Les Tuileries at 35 degrees centigrade in the midday sun.

With little persuasion we all agreed to head for the nearest café. I was unaware that the flock instinct could entice me into being a lily-livered 'yes' person. I was somehow persuaded out of my favourite gin and tonic and into a large glass of cold beer, which always gives me wind. But I realised, as I eased the weight off my aching feet, that these trips are part of self-development for your husband, your leg muscles and your self-realisation.

Back to the other half in my life. He was expected to return to the hotel at about 6pm, after his all-day conference with a businessman's lunch and refreshments. He arrived half an hour early and caught me sitting propped up like a wilting agapanthus in an undersized bath, trying to massage my heel to ease the blisters.

"So, shall we pop out and see a bit before dinner?" he asked hopefully, ignoring the drained look on my face.

I hopped dutifully into my leggings without so much as a whimper, plastered up the blisters and painted on a smile.

"There's a nice little bar round the corner, would you like a glass of wine?" I suggested weakly.

"I'd rather walk around a bit if you don't mind. Can't come to Paris and not see any of it," he replied with unusual eagerness.

We headed off at great speed in the direction of Montmartre, only to be accosted at the front door of the hotel by the larger than life wife of Mr Boss, calculatingly blocking our exit.

"Oh, my dears, where are you gadding off to? John is taking his nap. Would you mind awfully if I tagged along with you?"

That evening I was more than glad to sit down to a real French meal complete with garlicky butter, oozing cheeses and baskets of bread. This was better. This was what I had come here for.

"What wouldn't I give right now for a plain slice of meat and a boiled potato?" whined a Norwegian husband.

My jaw dropped in astonishment.

Day Three followed Day Two in much the same vein, but saw a gentle shift of mood.

When sore Sunday morning eyes met over the breakfast table on our last morning, we found ourselves recreating the hilarity of the previous evening at Le Moulin Rouge. And, you know, it felt as if the party had never ended. Maybe those bonds my friend mentioned had formed after all?

I must admit that Anne-Marie turned out to be one of the sunniest, warmest people I have ever met in my life.

Even the pink suited panther had a soft side.

Louise continues to run her Communication Skills Consultancy business in Norway. She works in the oil and banking sectors teaching skills mainly to engineers.

www.louiserankin.com

French Customs
Saskia van der Linden, Dutch in transit

The joy of cheap bus travel

I detest people who 'try to view everything from a 'positive angle". I once sprained my ankle and a girl told me to do just that and 'look on the bright side'. She was pretty annoyed when I replied the only advantage I could see was that I now only had to wash one sock.

For coach trips I'm happy to make an exception, and this annoys even the biggest optimists around me. Why on earth would I travel from Holland to England and back by coach when I could more easily board a plane?

One big advantage is, of course, the price. Sometimes a single fare amounts to no more than fifteen euros. That's one euro per hour if the coach is delayed by three hours... which happens a lot.

Yet there's more to my coach trips than 'cheapskatism.' It's the easiest way to move all my belongings, which are stored in a friend's garage. On a plane, it's near-impossible to smuggle in an extra bag because of tighter security, while this coach company is quite lenient.

Last but not least, I take a perverse pleasure in being

interrogated by French Customs, if I'm lucky twice in two hours in the middle of the night. Every time I end up being the most suspicious passenger on the coach.

"Why," they ask me, "are you only going to England for one day?" My favourite answer is that it's cheaper than going for several days. "Why," they ask me next, "are you wearing five sweaters?" Truthfully I always tell them that I am cold.

"Why," they finally ask me, "are you carrying these" – and they will point at the tins of *stroopwafels* (treacle waffles) in my hand luggage – "and why are they wrapped in so many layers of plastic?" It wasn't me, I keep explaining, it was that nice girl at the shop who also used too many ribbons and stickers.

Then they'll remove all the wrappings before they surgically open the tins and hand examine the waffles one by one, so that my friends would turn their heads in disgust if I were still to give them as presents.

What follows are a few prods in my stomach by a female Customs Officer. I so much want to tell her there are no drugs in there, there's only fat, but I find it wiser to keep my mouth shut.

In less than an hour, we'll board the ferry from Calais to Dover. By then, it won't be long before my friend and I give each other a big hug at the Park and Ride before we drive to her house, where I'll enjoy a long and deep sleep while I dream about French Customs.

So, I keep telling myself that that's all that matters and the coach trip was worth it in the end.

Born and bored in Delft, Saski lived in England from 1997 till 2005. She has a virtual relationship with Dr Phil and a real cat called Roxy.

Hello Dolly
Jack Scott, British in Turkey

Getting to grips with local transport

It was early morning and we were back at Bodrum's busy *Otogar* (bus station) for our final excursion. The little minibuses, or dollies as I christened them, buzzed about the cracked tarmac like demented bees. Bread-sellers, pantalooned grannies, cross-country migrants and lines of flip-flopping baffled tourists added to the scrum. Liam had begun his transformation into a bona fide plastic Turk. He stubbornly refused to let anything pass his lips unless it was authentic local fare and insisted on thanking every single waiter in dreadful pidgin Turkish. 'Turklish' I called it. His waking moments were spent pointing at random things in his line of sight, flicking through a dictionary and shouting out the Turkish equivalent like an excitable five-year-old on his first field trip. This day was no different.

"Coffee: *Kah-ve*. Bus: *Dol-mus*h. Bus station: *Ot-o-gar!*"

"Yes very good, Liam. Now give it a rest."

"*Tam-am.*" He grinned. *Tamam* (okay) was Liam's

definitive response to absolutely everything. Liam loved the *otogar* and would have stayed there all day drinking tea, talking to the trees and watching the crowds.

We beat a path through the raucous melée to an empty dolly with a Yalıkavak sign hanging from the inside of the windscreen, clambered aboard and sat at the back. The inside was sweltering and relieved only by a slight breeze sneaking through the sliding windows. As we waited patiently for the bus to fill, an old lady weighed down by capacious bags bursting with mandarins, tomatoes and aubergines, laboured aboard. Her bronzed, haggard face, criss-crossed with deep-trenched furrows was fringed by a floral headscarf. A hand crocheted cardigan enveloped her tiny body, stretching like a fishing net across her arched torso. Apart from us the bus was empty and she had her pick of the seats. The choice seemed to overwhelm her. She tutted, gestured at the driver, and shouted something indecipherable in our direction.

"*Par-don?*" said Liam. He smiled apologetically and frantically thumbed through his dictionary. 'What the hell is she saying?'

'Does my bum look big in these pantaloons?'

One by one, an eclectic mix of characters scrambled on to the bus, each adding an extra layer of colour: pale-skinned day trippers in hats and strappy tops; local likely lads in cheap jeans and gravity-defying hair held aloft by vats of gel; hirsute, beefy hillbillies in need of a bath. It was a heady blend that left us in no doubt that Europe, as we knew it, was a long way away.

The dolly scurried out of town joining the main arterial highway, an uninspiring road lined with commercial developments reminiscent of a sun-drenched London North Circular. Feeling like the Sunday roast slowly cooking in a fan assisted oven, we rushed past a hotchpotch of flashy ultra-modern showrooms, half-finished derelictions, out of town hypermarkets, ramshackle builder's yards and endless shanty *lokantalar* serving soup and kebabs. The dolly driver stopped now and then to pick up fares by swerving into the inside lane and slamming on the brakes. The rules of the Turkish Highway Code are clear and strictly adhered to: never under any circumstance indicate; always yell down a mobile phone when at the wheel; always ensure, and this is absolutely crucial, that you sound your horn loudly and often.

An expectant mother hailed the bus from the dusty roadside and struggled aboard. Liam leapt up and offered his seat. She dropped like a dead weight next to me, retrieved two onions from a tatty plastic carrier bag and handed one to me. I accepted it, assuming this to be a standard act of kindness and placed the lone vegetable in my man-bag. She took out a rusty paring knife, expertly peeled the second onion, quartered it and ate it raw. Out of duty and cultural sensitivity, I contemplated doing the same but quickly thought better of it

For the remainder of the journey Liam was the unpaid clippy passing cash down to the driver and returning the change. Eventually, he squeezed into a space at the front, in between a lemon-scented shiny suit and my onion lady. Live entertainment was supplied courtesy of an unseen passenger at the back of the bus, a woman obsessed with the distance covered by an *indi-bindi* (short hop fare). Her piercing and persistent protests were met by a robust sternward defence from the driver who feverishly waved his official fare chart to anyone who would care to look at it. Turkish arguments are loud, passionate, sometimes physical and ultimately pointless. No one gives in, no one wins, and no one loses. Our distracted driver was oblivious to the three helmetless teenagers snapped together like Lego astride a small scooter that weaved ominously in and out of the traffic around us. A disaster was only averted by an evasive wrench of the steering wheel prompting a sudden lurch of the bus. *Indi-bindi* girl shrieked at the driver and decided to vent her spleen by throwing figs in his direction. We all ducked for cover. When her supply was exhausted, the over-heated girl alighted. The dolly pulled off leaving our hilarious comedy act at the roadside. There she stood in all her glory, flaying her arms about like a mad evangelist, screaming profanities and rueing the loss of her crop.

Ten kilometres into our sweaty journey, we left the dual carriageway and ascended a gently winding road into tinder-dry shrubby hills, burned brown by the staunch summer sun. The choc-a-block bus laboured up the hill and joined a long convoy of slow moving heavy vehicles toiling towards a high pass framed by tumble-down windmills. As we breached the brow of the hill, we caught our first picture postcard glimpse of Yalıkavak shimmering at the end of a lush valley below, like randomly scattered sugar cubes on an overgrown lawn. This is where we would live, we both knew it. Who could wish for more? A beautiful town on Turkey's Aegean coast and rollercoaster bus rides with onions and figs thrown in for free. Paradise.

Jack Scott is a freelance writer and author. His contribution to Forced to Fly 2 *is taken from his book,* Perking the Pansies – Jack and Liam move to Turkey. *Jack has recently returned to England, after living in Bodrum, Turkey, for four years.*

www.jackscott.com
Blog: www.perkingthepansies.com
Twitter: @JackScottBodrum
Facebook: www.facebook.com/ perkingthepansies

Driving Me Mad
Jo Parfitt, English in The Middle East

Funny how it's never your fault!

My first accident in Dubai was caused when the taxi driver in front of me braked suddenly to stop for a passenger. I drove straight up his bumper.

"But he just stopped without indicating..." I stammered.

"You did not keep your distance," replied the police officer who arrived on the scene within minutes, shaking his head as he wrote out a bill for my fine and took away my driving licence.

He was right. But all the same, it hadn't really been all my fault.

That sort of thing happens every day. Many of us have arguments with kerbstones or traffic lights and I've often reversed into a skip.

Take the time my car ground to a halt on a Muscat roundabout. In an instant a moustached policeman on a motorbike drew up alongside.

"No petrol, madam?" he asked wryly.

I feigned shock. Actually I was shocked. I had been

oblivious to the bright orange dashboard light that had accompanied me all morning.

"Sorry," I whimpered.

"Pull over," he commanded.

"But I can't." I protested.

He hurrumphed.

I think he was more annoyed at my stupidity than at himself for forgetting that a car will not move without petrol.

Another police car drew up and two burly men pushed me onto a triangular traffic island before telling me to go forth and find petrol.

"Big problem," said my moustached friend, who shook his head, grinned, hopped on his bike and disappeared. It was 100°F; I was on the way to fetch my son from school and had a boot full of gently steaming fresh fish. He was right about the problem.

Fortunately, my helpless expression must have worked. A passing motorist drove me to the nearest petrol station to fill an over-priced empty water bottle with four star. The day, my waiting son and the red snapper were to be saved after all. I stood, fumbled and sweated for ten minutes until I discovered that the petrol cap on a Range Rover may not be removed unless the whole car is unlocked too. After eight years in the Middle East I had never had the need to put petrol in the car myself. I was used to merely lowering the window and handing both keys and cash to the attendant.

It can only have been another five minutes before I was able to jump back in, mop up my blushes with an inadequate tissue and drive off the traffic island.

In a split second another policeman, though I could not actually swear he was different, flagged me down.

"Big problem madam," he began as he drew an elaborate sketch of a car doing a U turn at the entrance to a roundabout and driving straight over the middle of the island.

"But you put me on the island," I explained.

"Me?" he asked puzzled.

"Well one of you," I replied, "a policeman, two actually, put me on the island. I had run out of petrol."

"Big problem," he grinned then calmly rode to the middle of the road and stopped the traffic so that I could proceed.

But amusing anecdotes aside, and we all collect plenty of them, there is a very serious side to driving in the Middle East and you soon learn to drive defensively. You anticipate that people will leap out at you from junctions. You expect to be carved up, undertaken or hooted at for no apparent reason. It is nothing to find another car facing you on a roundabout or to screech to a halt when an articulated lorry pulls out to block the road.

You just grit your teeth, start to use all your mirrors for the first time since your driving test, and develop a swivel neck mechanism that an owl would be proud of. You learn to think with your hands, head and feet all at once, to administer Smarties and reprimands while negotiating potential hazards every day.

But now and again you can't take it anymore. When one more person fails to give way and you are inches from disaster you can lose your cool. You toot loudly at someone who is quite blatantly in the wrong. The culprit looks back and shakes his fist. You shake yours back and point an index finger to your brain. Then he signals for you to slow down and talk it through like adults.

This brings to mind an incident, not so long ago, when my husband found himself embroiled in a similar semaphore argument. He swears he had done nothing to rile the other driver, but there is a chance I caught him taking his hand off the wheel and making a rude gesture. So there we were, driving along, singing happily along to *The Wheels on Bus* when he put his foot down rather sharply.

"What are you doing, Daddy?" asked Sam. Daddy was overtaking on a blind stretch of road, leaping two feet over a speed bump and turning sharp right, then left, then right again.

"A nasty man's chasing me," Daddy answered, juggling the gears and steering wheel with amazing dexterity as sweat dripped from his brow.

"What are we doing, Daddy? This isn't our house." Daddy did a handbrake turn and pulled over on a patch of sand in front of a large white villa.

"Quick, Jo!" he squeaked, leaping down from the car and pulling me into the driving seat.

In two minutes Daddy was crouched low on the floor at the back of the car in front of the bewildered children.

"What are you doing Daddy?" queried Sam.

"Nothing." said Daddy. "Mummy's driving now."

Jo Parfitt has lived abroad since the day after her wedding in 1987 – in Dubai, Oman, Norway and now the Netherlands. She has written a book year since she was 23 and now helps others to make writing dreams come true. She runs Summertime Publishing and Expat Bookshop.

www.joparfitt.com
www.summertimepublishing.com
www.expatbookshop.com
Blog: www.joparfitt.com
Twitter: @joparfitt @expatbooks
Facebook: www.facebook.com/summertimepublishing

Stick it Out
by Carol Mackenzie, Scottish in Norway

The blind leading the blind

After seven years of being driven around Bangkok and Jakarta, sharing a car and driver with my husband, what a relief it was to find myself in Norway, with my very own brand new car. Admittedly, we had to cash in the life insurance policies to afford it, and the wheel seemed to be on the wrong side. Still, it was a small price to pay for the freedom to stop at as many shops as I liked without feeling feeble. It was bliss to be able to sing along to my favourite songs too.

As long as the road was straight and had some other cars on it, keeping to the right proved quite simple; foolishly, I started to relax. Then I encountered an unfamiliar road sign — a yellow diamond on a white background. Of course, I now understand that it means cars entering a main road from a minor road to the right have the absolute authority to cut in front of you without even a glance in your direction. The brakes in new cars are pretty sharp, thankfully.

Norwegians are fit. Even pensioners sprint — onto zebra crossings cunningly concealed in front of junctions or around corners. My three-year-old daughter loves the excitement.

"Can you do that again, Mummy?" she calls from the back seat.

I regain my composure and re-start the ignition.

Roundabouts are a bit of a gamble. The trick seems to be to keep everyone guessing. Indicators must not be allowed to give the game away. Look as if you are going straight on and then suddenly shoot round to the left, scoring points off the driver who was about to enter the roundabout. Once you've mastered this technique you can move onto shooting onto the roundabout, thus forcing the car already on, it to slow down. Double points if it actually has to stop. It's a lot of fun and I think it reflects the egalitarian outlook of the locals.

The traffic police are very visible. I keep wondering if it's guilt from a former life that washes over me whenever I see a policeman or customs official. The first time I was stopped I was driving a car from my husband's office. Was there a red triangle in the boot? Was there any paperwork in the glove box? Did I have my driving licence? It was a bit of a letdown when he only wanted to check if I was wearing my seatbelt.

The second time I was sure I was about to be given a hefty fine for exceeding the exceedingly slow speed limit. Wrong again.

The third time came after dinner with my husband and my parents and a glass of white wine. The traffic slowed down, a road block had been set up. My mind filled with terror. I had visions of getting up at 5am in the freezing cold to layer my daughter in snowsuits and fur-lined boots to catch three different buses to get her to preschool. The shame of losing my licence and being sent to prison in front of my parents was enormous. Winding down the window, I felt as if I'd drunk the whole bottle. Of course, the traffic policeman spoke perfect English as he handed over what looked like a mobile phone and asked me to blow. I blew. I blew again. A green light came on and he told me I could drive on. I did, vowing never to drink again, not even in the safety and privacy of my own home. In Norway they test at the same time as the morning school run.

Winter came and everyone started talking knowledgeably about winter tyres. I had images of chains wrapped around the wheels of my car. Eventually, I forced myself to go and get fitted with some *pigg dekk*. The hunky salesman who'd sold us the car asked me to 'just drive on the ramps'. I gulped nonchalantly and got on with it. Mercifully, I succeeded and immediately panicked about how I'd get off the ramps with the studded tyres in place, never having driven a tank before. The studs looked like hundreds of silver pinheads.

After just a week in Norway, my daughter started pre-school. I set off in good time to pick her up on her first day. I spotted an old man in the distance and made a mental note to watch out for him crossing the road. As I approached, he stuck a white stick out in front of my car. Instinctively I slowed down, wondering if he needed assistance. In what seemed like a flash he'd opened the passenger door, climbed in and handed me a holdall. I looked down at the holdall in my lap and across at the blind old man talking to me. He seemed to be stringing lots of consonants together without the presence of a single vowel. Suddenly it dawned on me that not everyone speaks English. I hadn't started my Norwegian class yet. He continued rambling and out of the wilderness of sound I recognised the name of a local shopping centre. Off we went and I deposited him and his holdall at the door and sped off to greet Amy — on time. A few weeks later I picked him up again and took him to the centre of town. Not that my Norwegian had improved any. He pointed the way with his stick.

Summer is here. It is hard to keep my eyes on the road with such spectacular scenery. We drive alongside a fjord, the sunroof open, Pocahontas, Amy and I blasting out *The Colours of the Wind*.

Carol is now living in Calgary after 12 years in Scotland working in interiors. She is enjoying expatriate life, teaching ESL, and adjusting to life with her daughter at university.

Getting to Know You
Mark Eadie, English in the Netherlands

Some tips on country familiarisation

An expatriate is honour bound to see as much of the country as possible. Typically you know far more about your temporary abode's tourist attractions than the natives.

In order to fulfill this objective you need a car. In most African and Middle Eastern countries this means buying a four-wheel drive. With so many expert expats to call on it is hard to make a choice. Some people (mainly British) swear by the Land Rover Discovery. Others (mainly Dutch) swear at them. Whether your vehicle is made in Solihull, Yokohama or Detroit, possession of your 4×4 entitles you to unequalled knowledge of the ins and outs of off-road driving.

The second step is to buy suitable or unsuitable camping equipment. Hotels are rare and dubious in many such countries. Suitable camping gear is usually only available by mail order from the West. Unsuitable camping gear is available locally. When it rained heavily during the post Ramadan holiday in 1994 in Oman and

Dubai, thousands of expats discovered why their tents were so cheap. Again, when it comes to camping, the 4×4 comes into its own. With all that boot space we were able to take two kitchen sinks; one for washing up and one for paddling in.

The third step is to buy guidebooks and maps. The former are often hand written affairs, notes scrawled on envelopes or in notebooks. Maps are frequently considered to be state secrets, so the only officially sanctioned ones are on a scale that includes both the Equator and the Tropic of Cancer. Even when you have detailed maps, they are often of dubious quality. Maps in many countries are based on surveys done thirty years ago. Don't be too surprised when roads, rivers and towns no longer exist. On the contrary it is common for towns to be erased because of the presence of military bases or airports. As a result, guidebooks often contain no maps but have massively detailed itineraries, with instructions to 'turn left after 0.6km, then right at the orange bucket.'

Once the three key steps have been taken, the country is your oyster. In the Middle East, expats will travel for many hours, over rough and dusty roads, through monotonous desert plains, to reach a pool of water the size of the paddling pool they left behind in their gardens. If a waterfall is also part of the deal, it is remarkably easy to feel that you are a steely-eyed desert traveller, even though you are double-parked and surrounded by other expatriates, their children, dogs and visiting grannies.

In African countries, one travels to places where no one else has been, and preferably in someone else's car. Five-Star Relay will not help you when your car is bogged down 210 km south of Malaimbany, on a road last maintained when the French invaded in the 1890s.

One can find real treasures, and real disappointments.

After talking about visiting a famous bottomless lake of legends, west of Antananarivo, for over a year, we finally made the tortuous trip, climbed for forty minutes, to find that the bottomless lake had dried out and was being grazed by cattle. A few hours later, we discovered (oh yes indeed) beautiful waterfalls in a setting straight out of the Garden of Eden. Not for us the quick tour of Leeds Castle followed by tea and stickies at the Little Chef.

Several years later, we visited the Ain Hamran site in southern Oman. The local guide said that the last people he had shown over the site were the archeologists who had discovered it. This was all the more surprising when we considered that this impressive site was next to a 'tourist' garden and picnic area.

When it all comes to an end, and it is time for us to move to a new location (new country, new car, new camping gear) I find myself thumbing through the guide books and maps. I think wistfully of all those memorable trips Even the one when Tom broke out in chickenpox and Martha lost her dummy on that 1,000 km drive down to Salalah, seems like heaven now.

I always look forward to exploring another new country. Yet, as expatriates, we are not tourists, we are travellers.

I hope that in Holland we will find new untouched places — but hopefully this time somewhere with a decent road, a bar and a pool (heated, of course).

Mark and his family have lived in Africa, the Far East, Middle East and Europe, but are now back in England.

On Your Bike
Jane Dean, Anglo-American in the Netherlands

A love-hate relationship with a Dutch way of life

Think of something typically Dutch and the top four items will be, in no particular order, tulips, windmills, clogs and bikes.

Bikes will always be up there; they are an ingrained part of Dutch life and wherever you go hundreds will be parked up in cycle racks. Ninety-eight per cent of them will be the same basic old-fashioned design known as an *omafiets* (Grandma bike), with baskets of some description up front, panniers behind.

You recognize them immediately; the sit-up-and-beg gargantuans used by butchers and bakers with huge handlebars, Ferris wheels, buttock-supporting saddle, brakes (if you're lucky), built-in bike lock and three gears. These bikes are stately, solid, reliable and oh so comfortable and everybody rides them from *grande dames* to trendy teens, peddling along with ramrod backs and an easy grace.

Before we moved to the Netherlands from the USA we equipped ourselves with two-wheeled transportation.

With enthusiasm we headed off to purchase three flashy, 27-gear mountain bikes, so we'd be ready to explore our new country the minute we arrived.

The purchase itself was a daunting task as neither myself nor my husband, the Captain, had been on a bike since our teens. Harry, our then 13-year-old youngest child had been riding a bike from birth, so no problem for him.

Harry peddled off round the store having grasped the concept of changing gear immediately, the Captain in hot pursuit. I stood looking at the gears wondering how hard it could be. Back in the day my old bike had three gears — uphill, flat and downhill. The combination in front of me was mind-boggling. You had to engage first (I think) in one main gear then select one of eight gears within that combination.

Bloody hell.

"Alright darling?" breezed the Captain as he and Harry swooshed past on their third circuit of the store. Obviously not, but I'd figured it was a rhetorical question.

"Your bike okay too?" asked my spouse brightly, having been transported back to his youth in a matter of minutes. "Sure you don't want to check out any more, make sure that's really The One?"

Was he insane?

"No, it's fine. Really. Perfect. Honestly." I smiled enthusiastically to emphasize the point.

Back home Harry spent time each day riding round our subdivision in preparation for our move. There was no relationship at any point between my derrière and the seat of my bike.

Things didn't improve when we arrived in the Netherlands, mid-summer. It was only in the soft days of the Fall that the bike was pulled from the garage and used.

Lord I hated that bike.

There was no position where it didn't cause excruciating pain to regions you hope never to experience pain, unless it involves giving birth. It didn't matter how short the distance, I'd dismount feeling wretched and sore.

The situation with the gears was increasing my stress levels, spending more time figuring and factoring their delicate nuances than pedaling through, and relaxing in, glorious countryside.

The Netherlands is crisscrossed with miles and miles of bike paths through verdant fields adorned with the ubiquitous black and white cows, alongside canals flanked by windmills. I saw none of it. Between the pain in my butt and balancing the gear changes the bike rides were miserable.

I tried everything including the gel undergarments my hairdresser recommended; the idea being the derrière would have a comforting layer of gel between it and the saddle. It was a unique sensation but a complete failure in decreasing pain levels.

We invested in various saddles; bigger for more support; smaller to reduce the area impacted by pain, none of which helped. Eventually we discovered what I hoped would be my salvation. The blurb insisted *this* saddle was perfect for women, giving ultimate support to the bone structure of the pelvic area.

The Holy Grail of pain free biking.

It just looked weird, rather like a three-leaved clover. Two rounded mounds on the rear, one on the front and the whole thing smaller than a side plate. Balancing on it was one more stress to factor into a bike ride.

I have to say it did cause great amusement wherever I went; looking as if had been purchased from an adult store not Halfords. Older *huisvrouwen* in particular would give me very severe looks, and I'd see groups of teens pointing at it, doubled up with hysterical and obscene laughter.

The end of my relationship with that bike followed two incidents, both occurring within weeks of each other. The first was a bike ride with two girlfriends through the dunes to Katwijk, up the coast to the north.

"It's a beautiful ride," enthused my dear friend Susan, "it only takes twenty minutes, and we can have lunch on the beach when we get there."

I'd forgotten the dunes are huge; several stories high in places, with the bike path snaking up and down and in between them.

It took over an hour to get there. We found a delightful eatery where I could ease myself into a cushioned chair and the three of us imbibed several fortified coffees and a glass or two of wine — in my case for medicinal purposes to anaesthetize my rear for the ride home.

We emerged from lunch to find a group of holidaymakers standing round my bike chatting animatedly and pointing at my saddle. The conversation stopped dead as I retrieved the bike; none of them would make eye contact.

The second incident involved a ride across the dunes south to Scheveningen, the seaside suburb of The Hague. A group of us planned a trip for a curry and a few beers, riding home on a balmy, bright evening speckled with twinkling stars. That was the plan.

The reality was a pitch-black sky, no lights and no stars. The only decent light was the dynamo on Louise's bike and she led us home through the dunes. We'd only been riding for five minutes when my wheel veered off the path and was stopped dead as it ran into sand. The bike stopped, I didn't.

Two kilometers from home, whilst executing a complicated gear change I had ridden head on into a large prickly, very dense bush.

That was the last time I rode that darn bike.

I am now the proud owner of a second-hand *omafiets* with three gears, brakes, built-in lock, wicker basket up front and panniers behind. You'll often see me whizzing along, dog trotting alongside ears blowing behind him in the wind, with a beaming smile and a pain free rear. I absolutely LOVE my bike.

Jane Dean is an Anglo-American freelance editor and writer. She also chronicles life's challenges with a family of global nomads as Wordgeyser.

www.wordgeyser.com
Twitter @wordgeyser
Facebook: www.facebook.com/Wordgeyser

Holland on a Van a Day
Andrea Paterson, American in the Netherlands

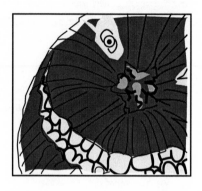

Halloween horror story

Throughout our time in Holland, our corpulent, gas-guzzling American minivan was a continuous problem. We could hardly have picked a worse car to bring to Europe, and I never stopped dreaming that it would end up in a canal. Even after two years, when my husband and I finally could afford a second, smaller car, we fought over who would get stuck with the van for the day.

Among the many challenges we faced as drivers of this car — narrow roads, fleets of bikes, blinding rain — Dutch parking garages were particularly tough. First off, there simply weren't enough of them. In downtown Washington, DC, where we were from, there are probably about 400 parking garages. In contrast, The Hague's city center has about four. As one comes into town, a helpful blue-and-white sign at the side of the road lists the garages and their status as either "*vol*" (full) or "*vrij*" (free), including the actual number of spaces that remain. If I was forced to drive into the city center, by nine in the morning the majority of the garages would already be *vol* and only some miniscule number, like 11 spaces, would remain in the open lot.

Once I arrived at the *vrij* garage and waited through the 20-minute queue to get to the ticket machine, I would have to navigate the impossibly narrow entryway. By folding in both mirrors and proceeding so slowly that my forward motion could only be detected on a microscopic level, I would inch my way through. Once inside, invariably the 11 spaces that remained were those next to a post or a wall and only about a foot wide in any event. If I somehow managed to wedge the van into one of those spaces, the fit would be so tight that I would be unable to open any of the car doors and get out. So my option would be to launch myself over the seats and out the back hatch.

A parking garage is also the only place I ever encountered a Dutchman who spoke absolutely no English. Our first Fall, shortly before Halloween, my two kids and I were on our way to the US Embassy to go trick-or-treating. (Because the Dutch don't celebrate Halloween, the Embassy attempts to re-create a mini version of the holiday with lots of candy and continuous scream sound tracks). Tentatively, I pulled into a Hague garage that, according to the sign, had a record 24 free spaces! And there wasn't even a line.

I proceeded toward the ticket dispensing machine and there was a sickening *crunch*. At that point, I accidentally hit the gas and cemented my car between the machine and the automatic arm, breaking off my mirror, gouging my door, and instantly flushing out the garage's elderly proprietor — a white-haired Dutchman in his late sixties.

"*Ga naar achter!*" he yelled at me, waving his arms and pointing. "*Ga die kant op!*"

When I didn't understand, he stuck his head in my window and continued to yell. *"Ga naar achter! Ga die kant op!"* Nope! No better up close!

Face flushed, he aggressively motioned towards the other entry lane. Inch by inch I backed up, as the man raced over to inspect the wall for damage and attempted to placate the other drivers already honking behind me.

After crawling through the other entry lane, I parked the car and we got out. I collected my kids — a werewolf in one hand and a clone trooper in the other — and we walked over to the ticket booth, my heart racing. I am not sure, but I think I may have let out a small yelp because the garage proprietor suddenly stopped what he was doing. His expression began to shift. I could see his mind working, processing this yelp, this universal idiom of a woman on the verge of a nervous breakdown. It was dawning on him that he'd have a bigger problem on his hands if I ran off screaming into the night. There was the faintest hint of a smile, and then he reached into a drawer and pulled out a roll of duct tape. After ten minutes, we had our first — but far from our last — official badge of driving in Europe: a duct-taped mirror, alongside the garbage bag over the window that would no longer close.

As time went on, we got better at the parking garages, but they never stopped creating a pit in my stomach. And we grew to accommodate them in ways that went unstated. Whenever visitors came, if I was in charge of the sightseeing, I took them to the lovely, historic city of Delft, purportedly because it was the birthplace of Johannes Vermeer and home to the lovely blue-and-white Delft porcelain. But my dirty secret was the Phoenixstraat garage — an entryway wide enough that it wasn't death-defying, and usually lots of spaces so I could hog two without getting dirty looks. Similarly, after serving for a year on an Embassy volunteer board that was devoted to building morale and designing outings for kids, I inexplicably resigned. No one could understand why and I offered no explanation. Oh no — it had *nothing* to do with driving into The Hague for the monthly meetings and having to search for parking.

We also found ways to give ourselves much needed breaks. One summer we took a driving vacation to Switzerland, and all of us fell in love with the Swiss Alps. The vistas were breathtaking: the snow-capped peaks cut into the icy blue sky, the cascade of trees down the lower slopes, giving way to the pale, emerald green waters of the glacial-melt lakes. It was beyond perfect. But the *parking* at our little town's train station... now that was truly amazing... big spaces... lots of room to turn around...

I guess, in the end, we learned to be more *vrij*.

Andrea Paterson is a writer and lawyer living near The Hague in The Netherlands. She is at work on a book about her experiences living in Holland.

Visitors from Hell
Susan Ventris, English in Norway

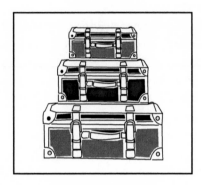

Why do your parents always bring so much baggage?

Picture this... The perfect visitors from back home arrive at your expatriate door. They're laden with bulging suitcases crammed with jars of Marmite, freezer food from Marks and Spencer and catering packs of Crunchie bars. They stagger beneath the weight of boxes containing a Fisher Price kitchen and a full size trampoline. In their hand luggage they've gamely smuggled six litres of spirits, then declare a thirst for tap water.

You love these visitors. They have their own hire car, and use it. They depart early each morning on sightseeing trips, returning at nightfall just in time to help the children with their homework. Their favourite meal is beans on toast, which they cook themselves. They're fluent in the local language and translate your awkward documents for you. They stay no longer than 48 hours.

These visitors are not your relatives.

Your relatives arrive with suitcases crammed with medications and a vast wardrobe for themselves, catering for all eventualities from Arctic snowstorms to blistering heat. They forget the duty free, then head straight for your gin bottle. You feel a brief flurry of excitement at the sight of a Sainsbury's pie, but its turkey and ham and you've been vegetarian for years.

Once on foreign soil, your parents lose all power of independent movement. One of these days they'll start following you into the bathroom. They never hire a car, or if they do, they're too nervous to drive it. They lie in bed until 10 o'clock while you sort out the kids and do the school run. Then they arise, raring to go. Each day they expect you to take them on excursions which leave you perpetually exhausted. Once home after these jaunts, their energy deserts them, and they flop into an armchair while you cook the evening meal.

They bring their medical histories with them. When healthy, they complain vaguely of the change in the air, but they're seldom healthy. They come armed to the teeth with medicines from Boots, but still manage to fall ill with monotonous regularity. If that bad back, frozen shoulder or gippy tummy is going to play up, it's ten to a penny it'll do so under your roof. Usually all three strike at once, and you struggle to suppress the natural resentment you feel when laced with an ancient Quasimodo with a severe stomach bug.

And they're forgetful. They forget about time zones and ring you in the middle of the night to tell you when they'll be arriving. They forget which side of the road to drive on, or they forget their driving licence, and can't drive at all. They promise to bring a recording of the latest episode of your favourite TV serial, but they forget how to work the video, so you get a documentary about the mating habits of wildebeest.

They have inflexible attitudes to food. Your diet of choice may now be vegan, or heavily influenced by the time you spent in the Far East, but for a fortnight you're back to a solid diet of meat and two vegetables. They look wounded if you don't produce a pudding.

Eating out is no alternative. They eat ruinously expensive meals in restaurants because they can't convert back. Educated in pre-decimal days, they know precisely how many chains there are to a furlong, or peck to a bushel, but are vague about the purpose of a decimal point. One friend's father ordered a bottle of wine costing £150 while his son was in the lavatory.

Their ways are not your ways. Brought up in post war austerity, they tiptoe around closing doors and switching off lights, then break their ankles in the darkened stairwell. They bath the kids in an inch of tepid water. They're too economical to hire a car, but surprisingly liberal with the sherry bottle.

And then there's the bad behaviour. Not theirs — although that's bad enough — but your own. One summer, driven to desperate measures; I sent my parents on an eight hour trip down a Norwegian fjord, armed only with a packet of polo mints. They were glad of these later, when they discovered that there was no food on board.

Parents are the worst species of visitors. You know they'll be coming back. The trouble is, we love them. So, for a fortnight a year, we put up with their foibles, discovering a few of our own in the process. Our guilt binds us to them. In our hearts, we know that no crimes they could commit while under our roof for a fortnight could compare to those we perpetrated while under theirs.

For 18 years or so, we ground rusks into their carpets, crayoned on their wallpaper, and roller-skated down their hall. Later, we played loud rock music at all hours and grappled with leather-jacketed youths on their doorstep, while they lay awake, fretting. The horrible behaviour of our own children is a chilling reminder of our own past sins.

Our parents, because they never change, remind us that we have. We remember that we weren't always this well-travelled, this well-paid, and this worldly. They're a yardstick of our success, a measure of how far we've come.

This is why we try to sound pleased when they ring to arrange their next visit: a phone call which always comes at three o'clock in the morning.

Susan Ventris is British and now lives in Perth, Australia, where she works as a naturopath.

www.susanventris.com.au

Another Suitcase Another Long Haul
Peter Gosling, an Expatriate Visitor

When your daughter only loves you for your luggage allowance

"I'm going to get married," our daughter suddenly announced.

Sighs of relief all round. We thought he was never going to ask her.

"And we're going to live abroad."

"Where?" we asked, our jaws dropping.

"It's in the Gulf," she explained. "Look, I'll show you."

She opened the atlas and pointed to a place that was a black dot in the middle of a vast sandy coloured area. It seemed one heck of a way from England.

"You'll be able to visit us," she said seeing that our faces had assumed a look of terror at the thought of our little girl being trapped in an oasis surrounded by camels.

"It's really quite civilized," she explained patiently. "They have shops, proper houses and an airport."

And so it was that a few months after the frantic arrangements for the wedding and the tearful farewells, the call came.

"We've got a nice flat and there's a spare room for you.

Do come, you'll love it. And by the way could you bring... ?"

That was the start of the lists that were going to dominate our lives for the next few years. At first it was just a few of the wedding presents that had taken up residence in our garage. Oh, and could we possibly cram some of her favourite tea in our case, and a couple of pork pies (impossible to get out there) and her Cliff Richard tapes.

Suitably loaded we set off and I must admit that what we experienced when we got there was nothing like our expectations. We were welcomed into the arms of their new friends and whisked off to beach clubs, fed in exciting ethnic restaurants and introduced to the magic of a barbecue at night in the desert.

Having developed a taste for the expat life we found that we were doing the trip twice a year and enjoying every new experience. Christmas Day on the beach in swimwear was certainly different from crouching over a fire watching re-runs of the Morecambe and Wise Christmas Show. The turkey and all the bits were familiar, but acquired a different character when served on a verandah hung about with bougainvillea.

Of course, each trip was accompanied by the inevitable request list, sewing machine, food mixer and the usual supply of foodstuffs unobtainable in the local supermarkets. There were times, indeed, when we seriously considered hiring our own cargo jet. But then along came the grandchildren. Or rather, the first grandchild closely followed by the second. Now our list of goodies to bring became longer and far more complex. Soon we came to consider ourselves as a combination of the Royal Logistical Corps and Oxfam. Children's medicines featured high on the list, followed by a selection of the products of that well-known chain store that supplies Lady Thatcher's undies. Still, we never minded heaving two trolleys of luggage across the departure hall at Heathrow. Very often, when I was so worried about our luggage being overweight, I was expecting to make the flight wearing two pairs of trousers and three shirts.

These were happy years, despite the struggle with bulging suitcases and long night flights, for our time as honorary expats has come to an end. Our son-in-law now has a job in England and they are coming back to live in their own house in the village next to us. Things will never be the same, but I shall still have that uncontrollable urge to stuff a case with food parcels and announce that we're coming to stay for a month.

This co-author of How to be a Global Grandparent *has never lived abroad but has visited his daughter (Jo Parfitt) and her family in Dubai, Oman, Norway, France and the Netherlands*

Christmas Preparation Redux
Linda A. Janssen, American in the Netherlands

Maintaining traditions can give you a headache

The first thing expats learn quickly is how essential it is to maintain rituals when living abroad. The second is the importance of a sense of humor. My motto is *'When the going gets tough, the tough get laughing'*. Little did I know just how apt that would be.

My maternal instinct and inherent grasp of the importance of celebrating holidays, made me the natural choice to orchestrate our first recreation of Christmases past in our new home in The Netherlands; that and the fact that I was also the only one who knew where all of the Christmas decorations were stored.

When we learned we'd be moving overseas, we had made a serious effort to downsize, culling out old, unused and unnecessary furniture, clothing and other items. Husband had a flash of brilliance and orchestrated a garage sale, with the remaining unsold items to be donated to charity. He enlisted Son and Daughter to help, and they did a marvelous job. Transactions were made, cash was earned, stuff went out. All was right with the world.

At least until that first December when we pulled out our boxes of decorations and our well-crafted, ten-foot tall beauty of an artificial tree that came with its own tiny white lights. However, the tree stand was nowhere to be found. It seems that the garage sale had been so incredibly productive that Husband had managed to sell the family Christmas tree stand.

Thinking I was dealing with a minor setback, I started combing shops and stores for a new tree stand. Daily I was rebuffed in my search, until finally I was redirected to the large house and garden shops; they often carry home decorations, and during the holidays are decked out in Christmas finery. I was shown the sole remaining tree stand in stock and purchased it on the spot, basking in the knowledge that a family Christmas was now ours.

That evening, while listening to the festive strains of Celine Dion's latest holiday music CD, Husband and Son put the tree into the stand. We plugged in the light cord, and stood reveling in the glow of the illuminated tree. Daughter helped me put on the various chains of gold beads and stars that we always decorate the tree with first, and then I went off to do other chores while Husband began hanging the decorations. Shortly, I heard him call to me in the other room.

"Uh, I think we'll be needing some new tree lights," he explained sheepishly, as I arrived in the living room to a dark tree and the pungent smell of burned plastic. "There's been a little setback."

Now Husband is an intelligent, resourceful man and having grown up in Italy as a teen, knows firsthand about the varying electrical currents in different countries. He had innocently plugged the tree lights into what he thought was a voltage converter (that would reduce the European 220 volts to the US 110 volts), but which was in truth merely a plug adaptor. Five minutes later as

Celine's angelic voice had reached a dramatic crescendo during *Oh Holy Night*, he'd heard a popping sound and started to smell smoke just as the tree lights went out.

The next day I trudged back to the house and garden store for white European 220 voltage Christmas lights. Since the Dutch abhor putting any nail holes in walls, I was also on the lookout for some wreath hangers, the kind that slip over the top of a door. No such luck, they were already sold out. Despite trips to two other stores, I came up empty-handed. It appears wreath hangers were as difficult to come by as a room reservation for Mary and Joseph at the Bethlehem Inn.

That evening, we finally had working lights on our Christmas tree standing proudly in its new tree stand. Maybe we couldn't hang our wreaths, but that was alright. We had persevered, rolled with the punches and figured things out. Best of all, we had our lovely Christmas tree and other decorations to help celebrate the holidays in our new home.

Fast-forward a year, and late November found me at our trusty lawn and garden center looking for wreath hangers. Proud of myself for having put a reminder in my calendar to do so, I waltzed in to find the last two remaining wreath hangers they had in inventory. Flush with my wreath hanger success and after prevailing over last year's trials and tribulations, I must admit that I went into that year's Christmas decoration process smugly convinced that it would be a breeze. Bad move. You know how they say 'pride goeth before a fall'?

Well, I fell.

The first surprise was when Husband and I went to the small outdoor storage shed where we stored our Christmas tree. Opening the creaking, weather-beaten door, we were met with a rather foul smell. Rain had seeped in through a crack in the shed roof, dampening the heavy duty fabric storage bag in which the Christmas tree was stored. Upon further inspection, it seemed that mold resided only on the storage bag, and not the tree itself.

I reminded myself continually of this good fortune over the next two days each time I had to step over the smelly heap that lay on the floor of our small Dutch kitchen. Why was it on the floor you ask? Because we had managed to misplace the Christmas tree stand that featured so prominently in the previous year's saga. In the middle of a typical multi-day rainy spell, leaving the tree outside wasn't an option. Hence my karaoke-style dance gyrations over and around the darn thing. Trying to put dishes away took an effort worthy of *Dancing with the Stars/Strictly Come Dancing* consideration.

I eventually unearthed the miscreant stand in Son's room. I do not know for the life of me why I would have chosen to put it there, but it seems that I did. I lugged the heavy tree stand down two flights of stairs, and we set about putting up the tree. When we tightened the bolts and stood back to gaze upon our lovely tree, it fell over. No amount of tightening worked. The bolt grooves on the nuts used to hold the tree in place had miraculously become stripped despite having worked just fine the previous year and having spent the intervening time sitting in a corner of Son's room.

The tree was too tall and heavy for the malfunctioning stand. Choices were slim as it was too far into December to try finding another tree stand. We could scrap the tree and go for a small real tree. But that would be too easy and make too much sense.

The tree's embedded lights were fried (given Husband's previous tinkering), some of the branches were permanently drooping (due to storage in a bag shoved into a shed), and the whole thing had a slight whiff of *eau de mold*. We knew the tree was on its last season, but being too sentimental (or too lazy, let's be truthful here) to toss it out and get a real tree, we chose the option of removing the heavy bottom third of our artificial tree. The top two thirds of the tree were short and light enough to rest safely in the broken tree stand without swaying.

Nothing says Christmas quite like a dwarfish, odd smelling, artificial tree to get you in the holiday spirit.

This is the part where normally we would put the lights on the tree and finish decorating it. Except that we couldn't find the lights. Yes, those would be the same lights we had to buy the *previous* year due to Husband's frying of the tree's original lights.

I know, I know, you cannot make this stuff up.

At this point I had already torn apart the house looking for the tree stand, and hadn't noticed any light strands. Husband wanted to forego the lights and just put on the decorations. Daughter and I, of course, were aghast. A tree without lights? Absolutely not. So, back yet again to the house and garden center to buy MORE tree lights.

Finally, the Christmas tree gods took pity on us and decided we'd suffered enough for that year. We slapped the new lights on the tree, loaded it up with half of our usual decorations, sprayed a little pine-scented air freshener, plugged the sucker in and called it a day.

Linda A. Janssen is a writer and American expat living in The Netherlands. She has won awards for her blog and is currently working on a book about emotional resilience in expat life.

www.adventuresinexpatland.com
Twitter: @in_expatland

The Horror of Holidays
Jo Parfitt, English in the United Arab Emirates

Sometimes it is easier to stay at home

It is round about March that expatriates working in the Middle East start to flag. The visitors have gone home and thoughts soon turn to the next vacation. As it gets hotter and hotter. 'Oh to be in England now that summer's here' is never far from your dry lips. It is not until you open your wallet to pay the airport departure tax that you remember all the things you promised yourselves the previous year. All those things you vowed never to do again. And here you are again. A glutton for punishment. Not quite as happy as can be.

Holidays take on a different meaning for expatriates who live in humid climes. For one thing, we go away to escape the sun, not to find it. For another, a long plane journey with young children fills us with dread. And to cap it all, the highlight of our holiday will be living out of a suitcase at his mother's. You know the story.

While you are folded up with your knees under your

chin, vainly trying to find a comfortable sleeping position in an Economy class seat, the memories return. You order another drink. You just know that your mother is going to blame your children's behaviour on your incurable housegirl dependence again. That she will smugly tell you anecdotes that begin 'when our children were young of course, we didn't have...' In fact children have always been impossible when staying with grandparents for extended periods, without toys, friends or familiar videos. But despite the hardships, you still wind up feeling guilty about that self-indulgent lifestyle you lead that keeps them from seeing their grandchildren. You try and point out that your brother, who lives in Balham, never goes home at all, but that, it appears, is different.

But enough of Granny. It doesn't really matter with whom you stay or even whether you have small children; holidays can be one long headache. When you live abroad for most of the year, the trip home becomes a mad dash in an expensive hire car with a small boot, on the slowest roads in England, visiting people who were simply dying to see you. You've let out your own house of course. It seemed silly to forego the rental income just so you could selfishly use your own beds for a month. So you lug your belongings round like reluctant tortoises on a marathon trek that leaves you exhausted, dissatisfied and cross.

You can't win. If you try to miss out visits to anyone who only wrote to you at Christmas, sure as eggs they'll track you down and ring you up. They'll make you feel guilty to the point where you end up saying. 'Sure, we'll pop in for lunch on our way down to Cornwall. We had hoped to avoid the M25, of course, but we mustn't let another year go by, must we?' And when you get there you have nothing to talk about. Their children are glued to their game boys while yours want to play in the garden. Your friends talk about the recession and unemployment and make you feel so guilty that you tuck your gold bangles up your sleeve and talk about the hardship of not being able to get Greek yoghurt in your local supermarket.

So you book a last minute package to the South of France and escape the recriminations for a fortnight, The hotel is in a dark side street and has no room service. Your sheets get filled with baguette crumbs and the bathroom smells of camembert. The children go to bed before you do, but are sharing your room. After lights out you end up sitting in silence on the bed watching MTV with the sound off. Or you lock yourselves in the bathroom, drink Export 33 out of the bottle and play Travel Scrabble. You also long desperately for some air conditioning.

By day you discover that you have to pay for the privilege of a rectangle of pebbly beach just big enough for your towel. It's not the expanse of sweeping bay that you can't keep your eyes off, but the expanse of sleeping flesh. After the Middle East, anything less than a 1950s one-piece looks obscene. And the water is freezing!

You soon realise that you can't beat the beaches back home. By home, I mean the Middle East, and after a few weeks in Europe you are virtually begging to go back. Even if it will mean that the steering wheel will burn your fingers and you'll want to strangle the housegirl, that the kids will revert to being video junkies and your friends will all be away on leave. Or will they?

Article first appeared in Lloyds Bank *Shoreline* Magazine.

Jo Parfitt has lived abroad since the day after her wedding in 1987 – in Dubai, Oman, Norway and now the Netherlands. She has written a book year since she was 23 and now helps others to make writing dreams come true. She runs Summertime Publishing and Expat Bookshop.

www.joparfitt.com
www.summertimepublishing.com
www.expatbookshop.com
Blog: www.joparfitt.com
Twitter: @joparfitt @expatbooks
Facebook: www.facebook.com/summertimepublishing

Stay a While Longer
Alison Day, British in Greece

When a holiday comes to an end

"Which restaurant?"

"The one in the square in the old town?"

"Where?"

"By the church?"

"Which church?"

"The one with the kiosk on the corner, where you buy *Karelia Lights*, before going to the beach."

"Oh, you mean Stelios's restaurant, with the delicious *tzatziki*?"

"Yes!"

This is the late 80's; after spending three weeks on the beautiful island of Crete in Greece, my money has run out and it looks as though I may have to use my return ticket to England. I don't want to go, I love it here! It's the freedom: working on my tan during endless sunny days and dressed in next to nothing; delicious cuisine and wines; Raki, the local firewater with slices of fragrant and juicy watermelon; a Greek boyfriend, and an international community that parties until dawn. I am sharing a house with my friend Kate, also from Oxford, and her Belgian boyfriend Luc, in the old Venetian style town, of Rethymnon.

The house is old, cool and dark inside, doors and wooden shutters flake green paint. Ascend a dark red, creaking, wooden staircase with ornate balustrade and you will find a sun blindingly white washed roof terrace, overhead azure blue-sky stretches to the sea meeting at the horizon. Other inhabitants in the house include, a Swiss guy, Tony, whose wiry tortoiseshell cat, Syriah, has just had two mischievous bright orange kittens. Then there is Cali, British, pleasant, blond haired, reads Tarot, her room is along the short landing from mine.

If I want to stay, I shall have to find work and Kate has heard that Stelios, owner of the restaurant with the delicious *tzatziki*, a stone's throw from our house, knows someone who needs help harvesting the olives from the family olive trees. Jet-black hair, white shirt, unhurried, he saunters out of the taverna, with two plates of the famed dish topped with a black olive, for his guests seated on wooden chairs at a scattering of little tables. Motioning us to follow him inside, we are introduced to a tall man, imposingly dressed, raven-like all in black, flowing robes, cap and long greying, curly beard resting on his vestments. He is Stelios's father-in-law, and a Greek Orthodox priest.

The conversation between Stelios and the priest is in Greek, which passes me by, I've only got as far as 'yes' and 'no' in the couple of weeks I've been here, but Kate can speak Greek. I see her listening intently and then start, her body stiffening slightly.

"What are they saying?" I whisper.

"Tell you later."

Negotiations finished, we follow the priest as he floats down the tiny side streets to his parked car; Kate and I jump into the back. Once out of Rethymnon the tarmac is exchanged for a dried yellowish-white dirt track with a light spattering of gravel, olive trees flanked by the reddish brown of the mountains in the afternoon sun. Any plant life left after the summer heat is scrawny and dried.

"So what was that all about in the taverna?" I glance at the priest to see if he's listening, he's not, prayer beads hanging from the mirror clack a dance around the green fir tree air freshener.

"I don't think he knows I speak Greek, but our dear friend Stelios told the priest that if we didn't work hard enough, he didn't have to pay us."

"What a cheek!"

We arrive at the trees, ancient twisted limbs, topped by small silvery-green leaves, fallen greenish-purple olives everywhere on the ground. A Greek lady has joined us, his wife, and tells us to put the loose olives into brown Hessian sacks; those stuck in the dried mud are dug out with fingernails. It's backbreaking work, and not made any the easier by the fact that we are both wearing jeans that are far too tight. Neither of us complains, we just get on with it, occasionally laughing at the absurdity and seemingly unending task ahead of us. Bored within minutes, I tell myself that it's this or England and slip off into my own little world of fantasy, occasionally jolted out of it by a voice instructing where I should pick up olives next, or those I've missed, deeply buried in the mud.

Lunch brings light relief, delicious homemade Greek food, bread, cheese, fruit and meat and the possibility to straighten one's back out. My fingers hurt; agriculture

I'm decided is not my thing. What a way to earn money. I can see from Kate's face that the feeling is mutual.

Later, the last olive is thrown into the bag; relieved we sprawl out in the back of the car to enjoy the ride home as our priest-chauffeur drives us back to Rethymnon. Along the familiar dirt track with the crunch of tyres on gravel and the occasional stone shooting up to clang on the car metal. All of a sudden, as if from nowhere, another car comes hurtling around the bend and runs smack into us. It all happens so fast there's no time to scream. Shaken but unhurt, we look at each other — we're in luck — a crazy ending to what was turning out to be rather boring day. The priest turns the engine off, snatches the key from the ignition and flounces out of the car, scavenger-like, black robes in full flight, swooping towards the culprit in the other car. Knowing the other driver is really going to get it now, we sit bolt upright on the back seat to get a better view, attempting to stifle our giggles. Theatrically, he assesses the damage and arms flailing, voice raised, he squares up to the other vehicle.

From the other car, another equally tall man imposingly dressed raven-like, all in black, flowing robes, cap and long greying curly beard resting on his vestments emerges; a mirror image of the other. Arms wave wildly; furious shouts attempt to establish responsibility for the damage. This is not passion, but anger and although we can't understand the words, its colourful nature leaves us as to no doubt of its content. By now uncontrollable laughter has taken over as we clutch at our aching stomachs. Tear-eyed, we discuss the possible outcome of the scenario; will it be settled by seniority within the priesthood, or could they be in need of some kind of divine intervention?

Artist, as long as I can remember; studied to be a Graphic Designer; became an Editor and started writing; gets paid for talking, as a voice-over; loves white wine and dancing.

www.alisonday.nl
Blog: www.alisondaydesigns.blogspot.com
Twitter: @alisondaydesign
Facebook: www.facebook.com/AlisonDayDesigns1

A Libyan Adventure
Lesley Morrissey, English in Libya

Expats sure know how to party

I'd had a summer in Germany and a few months in Belgium, but compared to my first experience of 'proper' expat life in Libya, they were oh-so-civilised.

I wasn't really supposed to be in Libya at all as I was, technically, flouting their morality laws, being pregnant and not married to the father. There was a certain amount of 'smoke and mirrors' activity at the Libyan Embassy in London to get my entry permit. I had no idea of what I was letting myself in for.

Landing gear down

We bounced down the runway in Benghazi late in the afternoon and emerged into a dry heat. My not-a-husband got us a taxi to a villa on the outskirts of town. This was not where we were supposed to live — in fact, if my partner had not already spent the best part of a year in Benghazi and known a few friendly expats, we would probably have been stuck in a flea-ridden hotel.

The usual occupant of the villa was on leave, but there

was a British villa sitter in situ. He seemed glad to see us and offered us a drink. Yes, really — every self-respecting Western expat knows how to make beer and 'flash', (something fairly lethal, very similar to moonshine or *pucheen*, and only to be consumed copiously diluted with Coke.

I discovered that the Libyans thought all our children were terribly healthy as we used to buy large quantities of hop extract! The alcohol base for 'flash' was shipped in amongst various chemicals masquerading as swimming pool supplies.

It was a steep learning curve and I blotted my copy book on the first day when I found a tin of corned beef in the fridge and used it to make sandwiches for lunch. How was I to know that you couldn't buy tinned meat in the shops and that this had been carefully smuggled in and was being saved up for a special occasion?

The expat community was very tight knit and the bush telegraph was extremely efficient. The next morning the door bell rang and I opened the door to find a cheerful New Zealander who introduced herself as 'Jan' and offered to take me shopping. As I hadn't yet acquired any Libyan dinars I explained that this would be impossible — but she said: "No worries, I'll lend you some until Peter (my not-a-husband) gets back."

She took me round Suicide Corner (driving skills in Libya have yet to be invented) into a couple of small shops with roll down shutters. I bought a strange selection of anchovies ("grab them while they're in stock"), tuna, tomato paste, vegetables and some kind of meat. There was nothing in the butcher's I recognised, basically you said 'Lamb' and they hacked a lump off a carcass, or 'Beef' and they said *Bukra* (tomorrow).

While we were shopping Jan enquired if I played Bridge. "Er, no," I said.

"Great, you can join the beginners' group tonight," she said enthusiastically. Little did I know that the main pastime amongst expats was playing Bridge, but I learned.

Expat gatherings

We became villa sitters so that when the usual occupants of the villa we were staying in came back, we just moved on to a villa round the corner to look after it while the family there, were on leave.

Jan recruited me into the Women's International Group. This was a highly illegal group of women from a variety of nationalities; illegal because any gathering of ten or more people was illegal. Colonel Gadhafi considered that a group any bigger than that was plotting a coup.

Mostly we only plotted strategies around the Bridge tables.

The social life was busy — if it wasn't a Bridge night it was a dinner party and various expats took turns in hosting these (also illegal) gatherings. Most of them were equipped to cook for huge numbers with spaghetti Bolognese and cheesecake high on the list of mass produced food.

Children were bundled up and put in a bedroom while their parents partied, then bundled back into the car and returned to their own bed later — often without waking. Sometimes, I was surprised that the right children ended up going to the right homes as they were usually extracted from a pile of sleeping bodies in the dark.

I live here

Life was kept interesting by occasional visits from army or police personnel. There were several varieties of police and you never quite knew who you were dealing with — civil police, criminal police, morality police or military police.

They made a practice of appearing at villa gates and announcing 'I live here'. One or two families were forcibly evicted from their homes and sent off to an unfinished block of flats some distance away, where their small children had free access to the open air — from the third floor balcony, which lacked a rail.

After a particularly bad eviction of a French family our neighbour, Richard, rebelled. Everyone gathered at his house to hear the plan. He was in charge of the fleet of trucks, including the water wagons, and had hatched the idea of pumping the water systems of the 'appropriated' villas full of cement.

Everyone thought this was an excellent idea — and much 'flash' was consumed. A record player (yes, really) was unearthed and the right disc found.

In the heat of the night a chorus rose from the veranda as the alcohol-fuelled patriots sang along.

"Land of ho-ope and glory, mother of the free ... la, la, la-la, la, la la."

The Empire strikes back!

Lesley was only in Libya for a few months, but despite the unpredictable lifestyle she has fond memories of that good old colonial 'stiff upper lip' and everyone sticking together in tough times. It gave her a taste for the expat lifestyle — and she spent the next 17 years in Dubai.

www.insidenews.co.uk
Twitter: @lesleywriter

Queuing: The Cypriot Way
Maria Antoniou, English in Cyprus

The waiting game

As Brits, we are proud of many things, queuing seems to be at the top of most things 'British'. We may not be big smilers or big talkers, but damn it we know how to queue. We have consideration for others around us. If they have been queuing before us, and we join another next-door queue and if the position becomes free, we would normally offer it to the person next to us who has been queuing longer. It's common courtesy, is it not? In Cyprus, 'the queue' hasn't been introduced yet.

My first experience of the non-queue was at the hospital. I had broken my toe and had to regularly go to the hospital to have the wound dressed. There was a ticket machine — well I exaggerate, it was a box with some cardboard numbers hand drawn onto them, thrown in this box in no order at all. Some people had numbers, others did not... a sure fire way of an 'I was here first, no I was here first' situation presenting itself.

I took a number, which resulted in many eyes settling on me with a look that said the numbers mean nothing. I later found out they indeed meant nothing. People just went in as and when they pleased. I missed my turn the first time I went to the hospital, but after that I learned to toughen up and if anyone tried to go in before me, I would say 'um no excuse me, I'm next'. The elderly members of society always, always push in. They feel they have earned their right not to queue, ever. It's happened to me at the post office, the doctors, at shops, banks, everywhere and you feel awful telling them to wait so they always get away with it.

A few months ago I was back at the hospital to go for a blood test. I walked in and saw a mass of people. This can't be for the blood testing I thought to myself. I handed in my slip of paper at reception and asked where I had to go. She nodded towards the crowd of bodies and said 'there'. She may have said to me, forget the next four hours of your life because they will fade into oblivion as you wait in a non-queue to give blood. You will have to fight and argue and shuffle forward till you get your place in front of the door. And once you get to the door, who knows, is there anyone behind it? They all may be doing more important things like watching the Cypriot soaps on TV, smoking, drinking coffee, gossiping about Maroulla from the canteen who was caught with Bambos in the staff lift Everything in Cyprus is '*Siga siga*'... slowly slowly, though sometimes slowly can mean still.

It's nice not to rush and panic, there isn't that frantic rush you find in London the moment you step out your front door, but when you need something done ASAP a bit of British methodology doesn't go a miss! ASAP – 'as soon as possible' in Cyprus it means 'As Soon As Petros comes back from the *cafenen* with my *medrio* (Cypriot coffee), I will read the paper, visit the toilet, smoke a fag, close for a mid-afternoon nap, forget that you needed anything and wait for your call the next day chasing me up'.

Maria was a city girl now living on the sunny island of Cyprus, having left the busy life of London behind her. She loves to write about the differences in culture and lifestyle she experiences every day.

www2.onthisisland.com/sections/the-cypriot-way

The Sauna Conspiracy
Ata Bos, Dutch in Finland

Naked competition

Every Sunday morning around 8 o'clock, I sneak out of the house for an enjoyable start to the day. While the rest of the family, or the whole neighbourhood for that matter, is still resting on one ear and recovering from Saturday night's partying, I drive down the quiet highway to Raksila´s public swimming pool for my weekly dip. Lack of time during weekdays, dislike for crowded pools and the need for exercise are main reasons for the Sunday morning visit. And, for the rest of the day, it feels extremely rewarding to stretch myself on the couch with a book and not be bothered by the image of myself as a couch potato.

Though I'm not the only early bird down the stairs into the water, the 50m pool has enough space, and I sometimes manage to find a lane for myself. After 45 minutes competing with unknown swimmers I drag myself to the showers, then up to the sauna. The pool in Raksila has fantastic saunas. Each sauna is approximately

16m². The concrete floor feels comfortable and warm, and there are tiny spotlights in the ceiling giving the sauna a cosy atmosphere. The saunas are clean and pre-heated by the dedicated staff. All of which is good.

On an average early Sunday morning I can roughly classify the sauna population in three groups. One, mothers with their offspring, who, I know from my own experience would most likely have preferred to stay in their beds. Two, the middle age crazies like me, who voluntarily choose to get up early. The third group is formed by elderly women who, for unclear reason, prefer Sunday mornings over weekdays.

It was only after a year or so that I noticed that there are some unwritten rules governing sauna habits. In Finland people enter the sauna naked with a towel in the hand. They come in, look quickly around and search their place as far away as possible from others. Everyone that is, except for the elderly. They almost always sit down on the bench next to the sauna stove, and begin shovelling water like they're digging for nuggets.

As soon as an elderly woman enters the sauna, I literally feel the heat under my feet starting to burn. To begin with, they routinely check and fill the buckets with water, positioning themselves on their sauna towel, between stove and bucket. Then, almost arrogantly — with a quick blink — they size up the other visitors. A wrinkled hand reaches for the sauna spoon, and I try not to groan.

Perhaps you feel I'm being overdramatic. Obviously you've yet to experience the sadistic, sorry, *shamanistic* effects. Like a Chinook wind carrying the heat of the mountains into the prairie, high temperatures force the 'thin skinned', the babies, children, their caring mothers, and the foreigners out of the sauna. I'm always wondering how long I'll be able to stand it. My Dutch skin, used to strong sea breezes, pouring rain and scrubby sand, can't cope with 80° C.

Every time a person leaves the sauna I feel the grannies secretly glorify. Within a space of 10 minutes they will, without a word, conquer the sauna for themselves. It's only a matter of pouring a cauldron-full of water on the steamy stones before the children, mums, and foreigners are defeated. One by one, as in the story of the *Ten Little Indians,* they'll leave the sauna to escape hyperthermia, leaving the old diehards in triumph behind.

I imagine that a whole collective of 'swimming' grannies will boast about new set records with their peers at Sunday lunch. Driving a certain number of people out of the sauna is one thing, setting new time records another. But beating foreigners at their age must be euphoric.

Born and raised in the Netherlands. Since 1992 on the move with her husband and three sons. The Sauna Conspiracy is part of a compilation of articles and short stories about my life in the Netherlands, Germany, Canada and Finland.

www.65degreesnorth.com
Blog: http://www.blogger.com/
profile/00125891487113523149
Facebook: http://www.facebook.com/pages/65-
Degrees-North/105983609429025

You've Got Mail
Ellen Weeren, American in Delhi

The art of standing in line

Have you ever been to a post office in Delhi? Stand in line with me as I share my experience today.

I needed to mail a few things to locations around Delhi, which is unusual. Most people here have drivers and so, more often than not, we just send our drivers off with the things we want delivered. And we sit all comfy cozy in our PJs while our driver maneuvers through traffic and crowds and runs many of our errands for us. It's lovely really. And yes, it is absolutely amazing that it is actually more practical to have things hand-delivered than to use the mail system. But such is life.

My driver, as fantastic as he is, does not speak great English, so today I wasn't confident that I could properly explain what I wanted done. You might think — really — your driver would understand the simple instructions of "take these packages to that post office and mail them". Really? Yup, really! It does not mean Khan is not a smart guy — in fact, I think he's pretty smart — but it does mean that I did not feel confident that I could explain exactly what I wanted done and that it would get done.

And isn't that lucky for you — because now you will know what it is like (at least what it was like for me) to go to the post office in Delhi.

First a little background — forget what you might know about the American mail system. It's a wee bit different here. For example, there really aren't mail trucks. There are mail bikes. Yes, that is right — bicycles. The postman rides through the neighborhood with mail strapped on to the back of his bike. It's not exactly the Pony Express — but it isn't quite FedEx either. You kind of cross your fingers and wish upon a star. Sometimes it works amazingly well — sometimes, not so much.

Knowing that I wanted these packages to arrive sooner than later, I decided to go to one of the Head Post Offices — rather than one of the smaller offices that most neighborhoods offer. I believe there are seven of these 'head' offices in Delhi. I went to the one near JorBagh. By going to the larger 'central' post office, I was hoping that I could cut off about two days of transit time from the smaller branch to the central processing branch; we would see how well that worked out.

Before I headed over to the post office, I tried to look up online some information about their hours, locations, processes — you know, find out when to go, where and what to expect when I got there. I never found a website that showed the hours; just a few sites that would tell me the postal codes for the post office locations. I am not sure how it is helpful to know what the zip codes for the actual post offices are, but if you need to know, you can find that online. Other than that, you won't find too many other (helpful) details. At least I did not.

So, I took a chance that they would be open today (Wednesday) at 12:30ish. They were. I walked in and looked around. There was a small window in the entrance way — but that seemed too easy — so I headed further back to the larger, busier area. There were several lines but I didn't see any signs that explained what they were for. And there were no 'take a number' stations. So, I got in the shortest line thinking that at least if it was the wrong line I would waste the least amount of time waiting. I am wicked smart like that.

In the way that I am very used to, I created and then stood behind that imaginary line that Westerners like to draw on the ground to politely wait their turn. Respecting the privacy of the person in front of them, and all that jazz. However, four people went up to the counter in front of me; one at a time, looking at me first, completely dismissing the fact that I might be in line, and then waiting for their own turn — now ahead of me. Interesting, right?

In the USA, I would have very quickly pointed out to them that I was in fact in line — I would have explained to them that the line starts here — behind the imaginary line — behind me — I would have asked how they didn't know about 'the line' — I would have reminded them that everything you need to know was learned in kindergarten — and I would have reclaimed my 'next in line' status.

But I am not in Kansas anymore and I really was not sure what was going on. I really, truly, could not bring myself to believe that all those people just cut in front of me. I let myself assume that they were all related — that they were there together.

But the seemingly new line was a wide line with people adding to it from both sides. It was not the line I know and love — single file, straight back behind the leader of the line. It was becoming clear that a new line was forming down the width of the counter rather than behind me and the shortest line had now become the widest line.

Then I heard, "Pssssssst."

And then, "Excuse me ma'am," and this woman is laughing a little bit — not really at me — but, okay actually, at me. She says, "If you want a turn, you are going to have to push your way thru to the front of the line. Go ahead and get up there."

Me: So, all those people just cut in front of me

Her: Yes, I am afraid so.

Me: You don't think they are related? Here together.

Her: No. I really don't.

Me: Is that really what just happened? They ALL just cut in front of me?

Her: Yes, you'll need to get up there. What are you here to do?

Me: I want to mail these packages.

Her: Speed post or regular post?

Me: Uhhhhhhh.

Her: Speed post is faster.

Me: Then I want speed post.

Her: You are in the wrong line altogether — move over here.

Me: Thank you so much!

Personal space in India doesn't mean the same thing as it means to me. Actually, it doesn't mean diddly squat. There is no such thing. The line was six people deep, but we were all within three or four feet of each other. It was a postal line sandwich. Smooshy. Twins aren't that close to each other in the womb. And it's still hot here, so sometimes people still smell a little fragrant from being outside. Holy, standing on top of me, batman. But at least I am in the right line — I know what to ask for — speed post — it's all good, right?

How did you know it was not? Did you read ahead?

Apparently that particular line closes at 1.30 pm. Good to know — except they never announced it — never put out a sign indicating who would be last. The guy just finished with the person two ahead of me and gets up and walks way. And it is frankly 1.26 pm. Not yet 1.30 pm. There is still time to help me for stamp's sake.

Then my little post office angel comes over again, still snickering. Not at me, okay, yes, she is still laughing at me. But that is okay — you can laugh at me all you want if you are helping me with this process. Laugh away.

Her: They just closed the window. You'll need to move to the next line over.

Me: You are kidding right? That line has a lot of people in it. Can they explain that I have been waiting?

Her: No — it closed at 1.30 pm. Just turn around and hand your envelopes to the man at the window behind you.

Me: There are at least 10 people in that line.

Her: Sure, sure — it's fine — just do it. Push your way through. Hand him your envelopes.

So that is what I did. I effectively cut in front of about ten people and handed my things to the man behind the window. No one complained. Actually I recognized most of them. They had been in my line but they moved when they realized the first window was closing. But none of them told me 'No, that wasn't very nice'.

The guy in the new window was kind of laughing at me too — in a 'you're a dingbat and I feel sorry for you so I am going to help you' sort of way. Again, I am good with that.

The postman took all my envelopes and asked me if I wanted speed post. Of course, I do, I said very knowingly — I think I was (not) very convincing that I knew what I was doing.

He stuck stickers on all the envelopes. Then he weighed them one by one and typed a good portion of the address onto his computer as to where it was going, calculated the postage, and printed new stickers. It took about ten minutes. The people in the line beside me all waited patiently, some had their mail out to be processed, but most just waited.

The total bill for about twelve 9×12 envelopes loaded down with flyers and invitations — $3. I marvel how that entire process can only be worth $3. I am not going to question it — but I am going to wish I may, wish I might, wish upon the first star I see tonight — that the mail actually gets delivered.

As I walked out, I once again saw my little angel. She was still smiling and I thanked her profusely. Thank God for the kindness of strangers.

Ellen was thrown into the expat world quite unexpectedly. She used writing as a way to chronicle her journey and as the cheapest form of therapy.

www.ellenweeren.com
Blogs: www.AReason2Write.wordpress.com and
www.AReasonToRead.wordpress.com
Twitter: @AReasonToWrite
Facebook: www.facebook.com/AReasonToWrite

English House
Sharon Brown, American in Vietnam

Because job hunting can be a challenge

My husband and I moved to Ho Chi Minh City, Vietnam in August 2008. My husband was beginning a job as a social studies teacher at the American International School, and I was leaving my job as a case manager with the International Rescue Committee to join him. We had long dreamed of living overseas and we were looking forward to our first expatriate adventure. After a month of finding a place to live, organizing our home and getting to know our new city, I was ready to start looking for work. My husband had settled in to a comfortable routine of teaching and coaching basketball; riding to work each morning on the back of a xe-om, or motorcycle taxi; and spending weekends with new friends, exploring Vietnamese culture and cuisine. I was enjoying our new life abroad as well, but I was beginning to feel lost without the sense of purpose that comes with working. I decided to seek out local expat networks to see if there was anything available for a non-Vietnamese speaking professional in the local nonprofit sector.

After two months of dead ends, 'Vietnamese citizen only' want ads, and a myriad of opportunities to work 'for free', I turned to the only field that seemed to be hiring non-Vietnamese speaking expatriates at the time — teaching English. With a rapidly growing middle class, English schools have popped up all over the country to meet the demand for a second language education, and because the need for teachers outstrips the supply of qualified ESL teachers, many of the less formal schools will hire someone without an English degree or a certification of any sort. Those were the schools that would hire me.

I was referred to a teacher placement agency called, 'English House', by a friend, and I sent them an email on a Monday expressing my interest in a position.

The next day, I received the following email:

> *Dear Ms ! I am from Englishhouse. Where are you from? Englishhouse company need one teacher teach Learningnet company. If you need, I will take you going Learningnet company meet student's. Are you free day? Thanks. Have a nice day.*

I replied promptly, excited about the prospect of a paying job.

> *I am from the US. I would be happy to meet the students. When do they need me to start? How many students would I be teaching? Children or adults? I am free this afternoon or tomorrow. What time we should meet? Thank you!*

Later that day, I received another email from English House.

> *Dear Ms ! Can you send me your CV ? Thanks .*

I replied, attaching my CV. That evening, another email arrived.

> *Dear Ms ! Are you free on morning ? Can you*

teach on morning? Thanks !

Still unsure of the age of the students or exactly what I would be teaching, I replied.

I am free in the morning. What would the hours be? What day do they need me to start?

I awoke Wednesday morning to another email.

Dear Ms ! I will call for you when they answer for me. Can you teach Wed on morning at 8 hour AM to 11 hour AM? Thanks.

Unprepared to teach that morning, but not wanting to miss the only opportunity I'd been offered, I replied.

I would be free to teach on Wednesday mornings. Would I start today or next Wednesday? Do you know how many students there are or what their level of English is? Thank you!

I got dressed and ready to leave. At 10 o'clock, a reply arrived.

Dear Ms ! I will wait and I will answer for you beacause Learningnet not answer for me. I new sens Cv of you for they.

Assuming that I would not be teaching that day, I decided to go out for a walk. When I returned another email awaited.

Dear Ms ! When was you born ? How long are you stay VN? Have you teach school ? Thanks.

I replied with the requested information and specified that I had not taught children, but had experience with adults and was hoping to teach older students. On Thursday morning, another email awaited me.

Dear Ms ! Are you free today? I will take you going Great kid at 14 hour PM. I and you meet at 765 Pasteur - Ward 6 - District 3. You will teach demo today. Thanks.

I put together some worksheets and other ESL materials I had printed out, still unsure of the ages and levels of my intended students, and set out for Great Kids. When I arrived at the day care center, I was led to a room filled with toddlers and told to, "Teach them English." They sat the children in a semi circle in the front of the room and placed a toddler sized stool in the middle of the circle, motioning for me to have a seat. Mortified, I sat on the seat and began singing the first thing that came to mind.

"The *itsy-bitsy spider* went up the water spout. Down..." Soon a chorus of little voices joined in. I led my little charges from the *itsy-bitsy spider* to *Old McDonald's Farm,* from *Row-Row-Row your Boat* to *Twinkle, Twinkle Little Star.* Fifteen minutes into my two-hour lesson, I had exhausted my store of nursery rhymes and was at a complete loss as to how to continue. Everything I brought was too complicated for little children. As I panicked, they sat in their seats staring at me expectantly, the nannies behind them looking unimpressed. Somehow I managed to fumble my way through the next hour and 45 minutes.

The next day I received an email from English House.

Dear Ms ! Ok, thanks. Today at 2 hour Pm, you no teach great kid. I will take you going to Learningnet company when Learningnet call me. Have a nice day.

Sharon Brown is a writer and communications professional. She has written and traveled throughout Asia, and is writing a book about expat life in Vietnam

Way too Many Balls
Nick Snelling, British in Spain

Football is such a great leveller

On the whole Spain is a benign country with a population notable for their tolerance and even tempers. However, the Spanish are also a passionate people with football an obsession, almost more important to them than anything else. I mention 'anything else' because on one raucous evening last year I think I discovered the 'anything else'.

Imagine, if you will, the scene: it is a sultry summer's evening and I am in the *Casa de Cultura* of a small inland village, the name of which I dare not mention. I am with a client who is of critical importance to a lucrative deal upon which I have been working for months and our negotiations, thankfully, are making unexpectedly positive progress. This is good news, as the lady concerned is British, late middle age, notoriously hard work, utterly humourless and something of an old maid.

The *Casa de Cultura* is peaceful but, as we talk, it gradually fills up with villagers until we can barely move.

Filling the room are widows in their black 'weeds', crusty, unshaven farm workers, stout ladies, stunning, doe-eyed teenagers and young men seemingly genetically linked to their sunglasses. The noise is considerable but I press on with my lady client knowing that there is but one opportunity to close this deal and success will mean that I will be able to relax for a month or two.

I look at my client, pretending to be utterly fascinated by what she is saying. In truth, I can hear very little. The noise around us has increased markedly and I turn around to see that a huge screen has been lowered behind me and a football match has started – Real Madrid versus Valencia. I prevent myself from grimacing, know I must concentrate upon closing the deal and turn back to smile at my client. She is droning on about some ancient back problem, her lips pursed.

"Absolutely horrendous," I hear myself saying to her. "Life can be so, so cruel. Now, about the... "

"*Oh, my God!!*' she screeches, her face going from florid to white in an instant.

"To live with such pain," I say, soothingly. "It can't be easy but in Spain quickly you will find the wonderful climate will..."

"No! *NO!*"

"... help. Truly! I assure you." I look persuasively into her eyes, but she seems totally distracted. "Within only a few months, in a village like this, you'll be feeling..."

"I ... simply... can't... *believe it...*"

"I know!" She is looking over my shoulder, utterly mesmerised. "But it is quite normal," I continue with determination. "Nothing unusual. In fact, most people don't believe this happens. But, I have seen it many, many times before..."

"*DISGUSTING*!" she roars.

Around me, I notice women shrieking with laughter.

"*Go for it, girl!*" I hear in guttural Spanish from an ancient widow close by. Near her is a middle aged man squirming in embarrassment, his face purple; a Real Madrid supporter, obviously. It is never easy when your side is losing and Real Madrid must be taking a real trouncing.

Nonetheless, I screw up my face wondering what the old lady could possibly mean by '*Go for it, girl!*' A goal must have been scored (which I have missed, damn it!). But '*Go for it, girl!*'?

A bit odd.

"*You can do it, chica!*" laughs a middle aged woman in a 'square lady' pattern dress, tears of amusement coursing down her face

A football match — and *chica*? Perhaps, I have misheard. Beside the woman is her husband who is positively squirming in his chair, his head in his hands. Maybe the men and women in the village support different teams when a game is on?

"This," screams my client above the din "is *outrageous*! I have never known... *anything... like it...*"

"Quite normal," I shout. "All part of the 'community' thing. An obsession but quite enchanting really and..."

'*ENCHANTING*!' My client's face has turned livid and now her eyes are bulging like a toad's.

Perplexed, I twist round to follow her manic gaze.

"*Oh, my good God Almighty!*" The vast screen at the end of the room is projecting hard core pornography! Two naked and rampant couples are in positions that I would have thought impossible. Meanwhile, near the bar, three heavily sweating male villagers are battling hopelessly with what I can only imagine is the DVD control, the channel of which someone must have changed accidentally.

Clearly, too many frantic fingers are trying to alter the

programme. The volume soars and the room echoes with frenetic pants and a sigh of raw, if rather exaggerated, ecstatic pleasure.

Suddenly, the screen changes to the football match, now barely audible. For a moment there is silence before the naked couples suddenly reappear, producing another bout of delighted shrieks from the womenfolk around us. The screen then rapidly flicks in quick succession to a children's cartoon show, the weather forecast, a pair of wobbling buttocks, a shampoo advert, a female head bobbing up and down and a wildlife programme focussing on squirrels.

Beside the bar the youngest of the three men now has the programme controller held in a visibly shaking hand. Everyone in the room is looking at him and the tension is palpable. I see him close his eyes and wince. The screen flickers: the squirrels disappear and momentarily a huge breast looms into view before, miraculously, the football match comes on.

For a few moments the *Casa de Cultura* is silent. Then, amazingly, there is an orchestrated, loud and very exaggerated sigh of disappointment from the women in the room, interrupted only by embarrassed male splutters. Quickly, though, the noise in the room escalates until it resounds from hysterical clapping, uncontrollable laughter and the pounding of tables. Knowing grins are exchanged, fingers wagged and decrepit, helplessly giggling widows are eased back into their chairs.

I look round for my client — but she has gone, and along with it any possibility of closing my deal. However, I cannot stop myself from exploding with delighted laughter alongside the villagers around me.

Once again, I bathe in the sheer charm of the Spanish and inwardly bless them for their lack of taboos and wonderful sense of humour. No deal can replace this type of experience and, grinning from ear to ear, I settle back to watch the last part of the game. It is undisturbed, but I cannot remember, for the life of me, the result.

Nick is a journalist, author of five books (including Taking the Heat, How to Sell Your Spanish Property in a Crisis, How to Buy Spanish Property and Move to Spain — Safely *and* Laptop Entrepreneur*) and runs an authority information website at www.culturespain.com*

www.nicholassnelling.com
www.culturespain.com
Twitter: @culture_spain
Facebook: www.facebook.com/pages/Nick-Snelling-Author/144711888902537

Housegirls Make You Fat
Jo Parfitt, English in The Sultanate of Oman

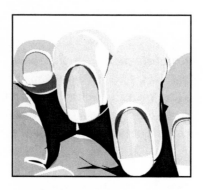

If only Julie didn't make such brilliant biryanis

Julie, our housegirl, comes from Southern India, and makes the most fabulous curry. Her biryani is renowned from Dubai to Muscat and popular demand has forced me to produce a small cookery book of her recipes. But it isn't because of her cooking that she is making, or rather 'has made', me fat.

Neither do I mean fat in the complacent 'I have much more important things to do than iron my husband's boxer shorts', kind of way. No. I have become fat from downright idleness. It all began like this:

"Oh you must have some help in the house," the hardened expatriate wives all chorused at the welcome drinks party, their perfect suntans split for a second by a sea of dazzling smiles.

"I don't know how I'd survive without Matilda," Suzanne said, shaking her head so that her gold earrings swung.

"There's just so much else to do," added Hazel, laying her perfectly manicured hand on my pale arm.

It was tempting. No more washing and ironing. No more windows to clean or beds to make. But best of all there would be a built in babysitting service on the doorstep for Sam (three) and Josh (one). Living so far away from the granny and neighbour breed of babysitter I would be bound to need a break. With some help in the house I would be able to write the odd article without one wriggling child on my lap and another asking why my mouse didn't squeak. There was even the chance to make a few pennies myself. It made so much sense that I found myself putting up an advert in the local supermarket almost before the telephone started to ring with hopeful candidates.

Troops of charming women sat, smiled, nodded and said 'yes, madam,' in my sitting room. I kicked shoes under the beds and showed them round, painfully aware that they were probably aghast at the current standard of cleanliness.

It seemed the right thing to do. The domestic staff who come to the Middle East all support extended families back home. The salary we were offering was like a fortune to them and I felt kind, charitable even, to be employing someone.

Julie joined our family, becoming Granny, Sister. Daily, Babyminder and sometime Cook. It took a bit of adjustment at first and was painfully obvious who was the most inexperienced. I found myself apologising profusely and walking out of a room if she was cleaning it. And I took to whispering in my own home.

But oh that glorious feeling of freedom: to explore the souks without having to steer an unwieldy double buggy round the potholes; to potter round the supermarket without trying to squeeze a week's shopping round two crisp eating kids who both wanted to sit right inside amongst the groceries; to go down to the club or a swim without having to take two pairs of armbands and a blow-up crocodile. And with Julie looking after the children, instead of my mother-in-law; I didn't feel guilty. After all, I was actually paying her. It made it all the easier to stay a teensy bit longer and enjoy a cappuccino in a pavement cafe. Then I wrote an article for a magazine and earned enough money to pay for more coffees.

Looking after children, carrying toddlers upstairs, scrubbing the floor and hanging out the washing had kept me fit. I had burned more calories staying at home than out of it. Sadly my favourite way of earning money, writing, broadened my behind more than my mind. But what the heck, I deserved a Julie. Living away from family, friends and fields deserved some compensation. I just slapped on some more suntan oil, met my husband for lunch at the poolside taverna and lapped up the high-life. Along came our club sandwiches — and the calories.

Hey ho, that wasn't so drastic. At least there was a simple solution. I left the kids with Julie and trudged off to the gym. Spent a few rials on the latest Lycra leotard, and started stepping, stretching, toning and doing unimaginable things with weights and lengths of blue plastic rubber. Once I stopped hurting, it was almost fun. Lots of laughs in the class, made friends. I splashed out and bought a season ticket. And just as the kilogrammes started to disappear so did my resolve. It must have had something to do with that coffee we always went for after the class. Or the croissant. I told myself I'd work extra hard to burn it off next time. Only I didn't.

I felt good. My skin was glowing, but the pounds remained. The ones that attached themselves to my buttocks and thighs, that is. The other, sterling kind, were slipping away like sand through my lightly tanned fingers.

Reluctantly, I unwrapped those same fingers from my coffee cup and used them for counting. I was paying for Julie, her visa, her bi-annual air ticket not to mention Christmas and birthday bonuses and gratuity. Then there were exercise classes and the post aerobic drinks. This exercise lark was not cheap. Nor were the latest Reeboks, leotards and floppy socks. And what's more to the point I was still fat. Happy maybe, but that cellulite was moving more slowly than my cheque book. For every hour in the gym I spent another 14 sitting on my backside.

I took the plunge and decided to spend yet more money. More an investment really, buying my own step and the video to go with it. Opting to cut down on both fat and spending — I would exercise at home.

The next morning I wriggled into my black body suit.

"Mummy, what are you wearing?" asked Sam as he lifted his jammy hands to be picked up.

"My exercise clothes."

"You look like Batman. Dinner dinner dinner dinner Batman. Can you fly?" He started to wheel round the room.

"Just let me do some exercises, darling. There's a video. I'll put this on and you can join in." I placed the tape into the player.

"But I want to watch *Pingu*." Sam put his jammy finger on the eject button.

"Just let Mummy do her tape first," I wheedled. And even as I suggested it resolved to add a second television and video to that burgeoning shopping list.

Five minutes into the tape Julie came in with the Hoover. Then Suzanne called to tell me about a ladies' lunch club. I couldn't win. Or get thin.

My house was spotless. The children were happy and cared for. The laundry basket was empty and the cushions plumped. I began to tap my fingertips on the coffee table as I fathomed what to do next. My long nails, unused to a life of leisure, made a harsh, hollow sound. Sacking Julie was the obvious step. After all, hiring her had been the start of my demise. But I could hardly do that, could I? My children would be disconsolate without their playmate. My husband would miss his biryani and another Indian would lose her livelihood. And I would shuffle from the PC back into the playroom and lose my source of income too. There was no going back.

I made myself a black coffee and took a celery stick out of the fridge.

Flicking through a magazine I soon found an advertisement for a local beauty salon. If I couldn't beat the system I'd have to join it. I booked my first manicure.

Article first appeared in Lloyds Bank *Shoreline* Magazine.

Jo Parfitt has lived abroad since the day after her wedding in 1987 – in Dubai, Oman, Norway and now the Netherlands. She has written a book year since she was 23 and now helps others to make writing dreams come true. She runs Summertime Publishing and Expat Bookshop.

www.joparfitt.com
www.summertimepublishing.com
www.expatbookshop.com
Blog: www.joparfitt.com
Twitter: @joparfitt @expatbooks
Facebook: www.facebook.com/summertimepublishing

The Carpenter Came to Call
Sue Valentine, English in The Sultanate of Oman

Some things seem so simple, don't they?

The recipe books were too numerous for the space they held on the counter, somewhere between the cooker and the sink. The books had been preventing me from serving up a meal onto four plates for several weeks and had recently acquired the habit of sliding sideways like dominoes in the wake of regular kettle floods. I needed a shelf; time then, to call a carpenter.

Easy, you would think. But I live in a Middle Eastern country where the workmen tend to be paid little and are rarely fluent in English. A place where houses are all rented and we are told that all communication with the landlord must come from a male.

So, I asked my husband to ask the maintenance man to ask the carpenter to telephone and make an appointment.

The following day the carpenter called round at the house himself unannounced. I was out, of course.

"When did he say he would come back?" I asked Roti, our housegirl.

"He didn't say ma'am."

Oh well, start again. This time I asked my husband to ask the maintenance man for the carpenter's telephone number.

I broke with convention and called the carpenter myself. He arrived at the appointed time.

I gave him a drawing and explained what was required — a fatal mistake. Never try to explain when there is a language barrier. It just gives you a false sense of security because you invariably receive smiles and nods in reply, which unfortunately do not mean 'yes', but instead "I am very friendly and willing and would like to please you but don't understand a word you are saying."

The carpenter took out his retractable tape-measure and measured. Twice. He failed to write anything down.

I asked him if he fully understood. Yes, you've guessed it, he nodded and smiled and said "yes madam."

Time passed. The pages of my cookery books were crinkled and glued together from a mixture of water and spilled gravy. I asked my husband to call the maintenance man who would, in turn, call the carpenter. Nothing. I asked my husband to call the carpenter. Still nothing. In the end I called the carpenter myself. I called the maintenance man myself. In time the carpenter did indeed reappear with the shelf, sorry that is not strictly true: he returned with a shelf.

It was the correct length — an amazing feat when you consider he had only to rely on his memory. It was round about the right width too — nothing short of a miracle. But the wood was rough and unpainted and there was not a bracket in sight.

I asked about the supports of course. I pointed at my copy of the original drawing, which clearly showed brackets.

"Coming, madam," he replied and nodded and smiled some more.

I asked about the rough wood

"We are painting, madam," he assured.

True to his word, later that day, the carpenter's friend and his assistant arrived with a tin of paint. Three men with wide brushes painted my narrow shell, then stood it on its wet end in the middle of my patio and went away.

Three days later they returned triumphantly with the supports. I think they wanted to impress me for they had already been painted. A different colour.

Eventually, the damage done to the paintwork, which had been caused by the less than clean concrete on which it had stood, was repaired. They even corrected the discrepancy in the colour. They attached it to the wall using the brackets. At just the second attempt it was straight — once I had suggested they borrow our spirit-level.

A year later, the shelf still stands. But today, when *Delia Smith's Christmas* flopped down into my flapjack, I came to the stark realisation that my cookery books have been at it again. They have been multiplying without my consent. I guess it's time to get my husband to call the maintenance man to call that carpenter again. Or maybe I'll do it myself this time?

Sue enjoys writing, photography and travel. She is a qualified food scientist, works in food safety and product development and co-authored a cookbook called Dates. *She is now in England but has lived in Oman and India. Sue is married with two sons.*

All Part of the Service
Jo Parfitt, English in Norway

Are service engineers all they are cracked up to be?

I have just had an extremely interesting conversation with a Norwegian washing machine engineer about my spin cycle. Subsequent to my initial request he called me on his mobile phone and left a perfectly coherent message on my answering machine. He said he would come at noon. He did. He took away my washing machine and promised to deliver it the next day.

After eight years in the Middle East I can tell you it is a rare comfort to know that my electrical appliances are in safe hands. I spent years perfecting the art of shouting bald statements down an unfriendly telephone to the tune of 'Dishwasher broken. Problem. Come. Please. Now.' Only to know that the next step would be giving instructions to find my house. The following step would be to give the same instructions again. The next to ask if he had a pencil. Finally, I would wait home all the next day and he would not turn up. Then when he did finally appear, there would be several smiling gentlemen considerately leaving their flip-flops on my doorstep followed by a lot of head shaking, a few bangs with a hammer, and then a desolate cry of, "It is broken, Madam." Which, of course, I knew. Then they would troop off for a van, which would appear unannounced during the following week and then that would be the end of my dishwasher until I had found a way through a labyrinth of the service centre's telephone system to a man who always promised 'tomorrow In Shallah' and then asked my name.

I could bore you with endless examples of my experience with service engineers, none of which ever seemed amusing at the time, but in retrospect are infinitely so. But let me just share some of the juiciest.

Like the time our washing machine tripped the electricity in the entire house every time it started to spin. I needed to stand on the freezer in order to reach the trip switch. The freezer and trip switch were kept in the store room — the only area of the house without natural light. So, I would blindly fumble and climb in the dark, find the switch, only to be blasted back into darkness the moment the spin reached its peak again; usually when I had just closed the store room door.

I wish there had been a happy ending to the story, but sadly it went from bad to worse. The tripping got so bad that we called in the experts. An expert left his flip-flops on the door mat, balanced himself on the freezer and accidentally put two of the wrong wires together. There was a rather loud bang. From the office where my husband and I sat calmly tapping away at our keyboards we took our eyes off the screens and shrugged at each other, presuming the expert had fallen off the freezer. Then we saw smoke pouring out of the fax machine. Our computers died and all round the house similar fumes poured from the video, television and all electrical appliances that used power supplies.

"No problem," said the expert, poking his dark fringe from his eyes with his screwdriver.

"Big problem," we replied and calmly waved goodbye to several hundred pounds, replacing our power supplies and repairing our technology reliant life.

The expert scuttled off and we called in a man from the Ministry of Electricity and Water. He told us that we had 37 take offs when we should only have had 16 and went away to make his report. It never came but the landlord scuttled round with his tail between his legs and made our electricity safe for the first time in 17 years. Meanwhile our neighbours told us of the time their own store room had actually caught fire owing to the same problem.

Then there was the time our water was cut off for non payment of bills (plural). Yet we had never received one. The housegirl had a vague recollection of a brown envelope being thrown over the garden wall. The man at the Ministry reckoned that must have been the bill and told us to go and check our water meter in the garden. We did. It had gone.

"Oh yes," said the man at the Ministry, "You didn't pay the bill."

He promised to send a man. He sent several. Led by an Iranian and with a collection of Omanis. Pakistanis and Indians in tow, they left their sandals by the front door, went out of the back and into the garden barefoot.

"Your meter has gone!" they declared.

My husband made an irate phone call at midnight. It was midsummer and without water the house was starting to smell. He was summoned to see a Minister the following morning and urged to bring cash for the unpaid bills.

At almost exactly the time water again coursed through our parched pipework, Ian was outside the Minister's office waiting to be summoned, the rials weighing heavy in his pocket. The Minister just wanted to make us sweat for our water.

Of course there was the time when we had too much water. It all began when a workman dug through the main water pipe line in the park and cut off most of Muscat. With amazing efficiency, the blue water lorries, usually used to service the houses that are not yet connected to the mains, jumped into action. Within a few hours our small estate had two such lorries ready and able to fill our tanks through the pipes that had now rusted superbly from lack of use. The driver leapt down from his cab, connected the nozzle to our rusty pipe and started to chat. A few minutes later a blood red waterfall cascaded noisily from the water tank under the roof to the basement of our four-floored villa. The driver cocked his head to one side.

"No problem," he said flatly. "That happened next door too." And he jumped back into his cab ready to flood his next unsuspecting victim.

Maintenance men are full of surprises too. Our most recent was called Ravi and it always amazed us that in three years, no one at his office ever seemed to know who we were talking about when we phoned. He redeemed himself with a moment of glory involving a snake.

The aforementioned snake had slithered into the playroom through a slit in the top of one of the doors. An obliging Sri Lankan maid, with more guts than I, launched at it with a broom and blithely bunged it in a plastic bag. Ravi came along surprisingly quickly, armed with an odd shaped piece of wood and some nails and neatly banged it into place, over the gap at the top of the offending French door. We never could use the door again.

Service takes on another meaning when you are in a foreign country. 'Immediately' is often translated as 'soon' while 'urgent' jobs are relegated to the end of the queue. The day you have planned a weekend away the car mechanic goes sick and your four-wheel-drive is left unmended and forlorn. Taxis have no A to Z and fail to find your house when you need to go to the airport. To prevent an airport no-show you have to pick a taxi earlier in the day on a recce to your house. Then he has a good chance of actually finding his way back later to take you to your flight.

When we needed a plumber to sort out a blockage in our top floor lavatory we were naturally rather embarrassed. But our red faces fell as we watched him descend the stairs with the 'blockage' dripping from a plastic grocery bag.

Some service people are punctual and efficient, many are not. We became accustomed to shouting instructions, faxing maps and waiting impatiently for Mr Fix-its who either couldn't fix-it or never appeared at all. We saw tree fellers balance on the very branch they were slicing. We knew service to come with a smile, but never exactly as we'd hoped.

Today I am still reeling from the shock that my washing machine is to be mended within 24 hours of my call.

I can't believe that the Norwegian who is fixing it speaks perfect English and came at the appointed time. But it made me feel secure to see that he too left sandals on the doormat.

Jo Parfitt has lived abroad since the day after her wedding in 1987 – in Dubai, Oman, Norway and now the Netherlands. She has written a book year since she was 23 and now helps others to make writing dreams come true. She runs Summertime Publishing and Expat Bookshop.

www.joparfitt.com
www.summertimepublishing.com
www.expatbookshop.com
Blog: www.joparfitt.com
Twitter: @joparfitt @expatbooks
Facebook: www.facebook.com/summertimepublishing

Hairdressers Make Your Toes Curl
Linda March, English in Norway

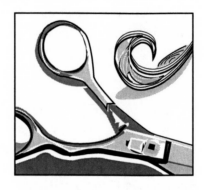

Now you have reason to be terrified of strange hairstylists

Three months into our first experience of expatism in an excruciatingly expensive Scandinavian country, I was beginning to learn the ropes. I had driven up snowy mountains, learned how to 'coffee morning' and how to feel uneasy on entering a supermarket with less than £100 in my purse. In other words I had everything sussed — well almost everything. I had yet to find the courage to visit a hairdresser.

My reluctance to take the plunge was born out of two things. Firstly, my attachment to my hairdresser back home: Helen and I had been together for over eight years. She'd seen me through a tricky moment with a floral hair piece on my wedding day. She'd given me the pregnancy-manual-recommended trim, two weeks before the due date of my first child, so I'd still look good when pushing and panting and entertaining visitors (well, okay, even Helen couldn't do the impossible). She'd sympathised with my post-natal hair loss and found enterprising ways to make less look more, and, most importantly, during the last four years, she'd been supporting me through the trauma of greyness with a large bottle of vegetable dye. Nobody could take her place. Nobody. Secondly, I'd been warned about the local hairdressers by several people. Not only did they charge frightening amounts of money to trim a child's fringe, but they did not take kindly to being told what to do. In addition, I'd heard that they tended to specialise in one style and that you came out with that style, regardless of your preference. The only solution seemed to be to hang around outside all the hairdressers in town until I found one with people emerging in a style I favoured.

By Christmas things were desperate and we were all very shaggy indeed. However, it seemed that help was at hand in the form of Damir, John's Bosnian friend. Damir had a friend called Vanessa who had been a hairdresser back in Mostar. Her qualifications weren't recognised in Norway so she worked from home on the black economy, styling the hair of all the local refugees.

I asked John about Damir's wife's hair and he said it was 'fine'. Of course, this was a foolish question, as his judgement on women's hairstyles is not something I had ever considered valuing before. In fact, when pressed, he could describe neither style nor colour, but maintained it was definitely 'fine'.

Anxious, but with vision rapidly declining, I agreed to take the plunge and we all trooped off to Vanessa's. We stopped on the way to collect Damir, so that he could show us the way, introduce us, and perform a more important role as we were later to discover.

Vanessa's little flat was rather sad. It was our first glimpse of anything less than wealth here. All her possessions were on two shelves against the wall in a bare sitting room. But the atmosphere was cheerful enough as several Bosnians were drinking strong coffee and chatting noisily.

The 'salon' was a tiny room bearing a white plastic garden chair and a mirror placed just too high on the wall to be of any use to the clients. As usual, my older daughter had to be first and she plonked herself in the chair. It was now that we discovered Damir's role — no, not sweeping up the hair trimmings — interpreting!

Being rather a reserved person and used to the unwritten law of confidentiality between a woman and her coiffeuse, I had never discussed my hairdressing requirements in the presence of my husband, far less several interested Bosnian strangers. I began to panic as I wondered whether Damir's excellent engineering English was up to his ladies' hairdressing English. My terse 'just a trim' took about five minutes to translate and was accompanied by all manner of Bosnian hand waving. I had failed to notice that he and Vanessa's husband had the shortest hair ever seen on a non-bald person and I hoped that three years in this new land hadn't rubbed off on Vanessa and made her start practising only that one style.

I need not have worried. She made a good job of the children's hair and I drank very strong, very sweet coffee, while wondering how I looked and waiting for John to emerge. Like many ex-servicemen of his generation, he has spent the last ten years making up for having been condemned to a short back and sides at a time when the rest of the youth of the western world had boasted long locks flowing halfway down their backs. Since then, although his leg is often pulled about it, his longish curly hair has been his trade mark. Or should I say 'had been'.

It seems strange that Damir's excellent command of English did not extend to 'not too short' or maybe my fears of the one style were well founded. The wicked grin that Damir exchanged with his friends may hold the answer.

When my shorn and downcast husband emerged, our children fell off their chairs laughing at his ears, of which they had been in blissful ignorance until that moment. Whilst I reflected on the sad loss of childhood innocence, Damir informed us of the amazingly low cost of this adventure.

As John will now only need his hair cutting once a year, we should be quids in.

When not helping others make an impact with their written words through her proofreading and editing work, Linda is working on a novel and family history.

www.goodenglishcompany.com

Departures

"I never know whether to call the packers or the divorce lawyer."

Clare Ashley, after nine moves in six years.

"I'm so used to getting a week's notice that I can't cope this time, now we have had a month to think about things. I'm panicking!"

Fiona Lonsdale, after ten moves in ten years.

"My husband always tells me not to hang up new curtains. He knows that the moment I make that step we will hear of our next posting."

Véronique Kampmann, wife of Chief Executive Geco Prakla.

"I was pleased to be returning to a real life and country with fresh air and seasons, long-standing friends and family."

Susan Valentine, after The Sultanate of Oman.

"Departing fills me with dread and sadness at leaving such a beautiful, majestic country, which is still filled with communities. I fear the rut of English routine, which might replace my Great Adventure. I'd feel I'd given in."

Christine Yates, paling at the thought of leaving Germany.

"I left with mixed feelings. Saying goodbye to a tax-free salary is never easy. On the other hand, when you've climbed every mountain, skied every piste and eaten every Toblerone, then the time comes when you have to move on to new pastures."

Paul Cleary, after Switzerland.

"It feels like you have just seen an epic film or read a long book, where you became very involved. Great while it lasted and well worth it, but not something you would want to go through again."

Alice Hurley, after Norway and the USA.

"I did not miss those cliques, that gossip and the way we had lived in each other's pockets."

Colleen Macdonald, after Trinidad.

Life without the Cleaners: the real dirt
Susie Csorsz Brown, American in America

The worst thing about going home

For the first time in more than a decade, I am going to have to clean the house all by myself. OMG. How does one live without someone else to clean up after the messes the male portion of this herd generates? Beyond the minimal keep-the-floor-quasi-clean, I haven't done much cleaning since we first went overseas 10 years ago. Even when we have come back to the States, we've lived in serviced apartments. The thought of this is kind of overwhelming.

I know that kind of makes me sound like a whiny, spoiled girl. I'm not really. Most people would describe me as a bit compulsive, and mostly organized. I've always done the laundry, though, and always do the clean-up after cooking and dinner. But all of the sheets, and floors, and bathrooms, and dusting, and laundry cooking... seriously, OMG!

I am looking forward to getting to be the one that washes the towels. I get to be the one that doesn't put softener in with the towels, so when we use the towels they actually take the water off our bodies; which doesn't happen when softener is used. There is nothing quite as annoying as finding oneself just as dripping wet AFTER toweling off as before.

It used to be that I used to clean the house before the cleaner came. I couldn't help myself. Here was this nice woman, coming into my home. Surely, I couldn't leave a big mess for her, right? My husband used to just shake his head, saying I was doing her job for her. He'd tell other people at lunch the next day, and they all nodded sympathetically, "New girl. She'll get used to it." We shared that particular housekeeper with another family, and they very obviously did not have the same must-clean-the-house-quick issues that I did. I think the housekeeper started to regard her time at our house as her vacation time. This was probably around the same time she decided that she was my best friend, and would regale me with her previous housecleaning escapades, astonishing me with her confessions. I was getting a lesson in how not to be the boss, and I was failing miserably.

In my defense, I didn't grow up with a housekeeper. We had chores. If we didn't do them, we didn't get our allowance. It wasn't a given that someone else would come and clean our house, like it is overseas. Overseas, you are expected to 'share the wealth,' regardless of how uncomfortable you may or may not be with the idea. So my husband continued to shake his head at me every day through two tours, until I finally got more accustomed to someone else coming in to clean up my messes; and grew to like it. It was so much easier, sharing the workload with someone else.

My kids have had no trouble getting used to others cleaning up after them. Have you ever seen the destruction three boys can bring upon a room? Holy cow. I now had to reverse my thinking and start cleaning up for the staff again, but this time, I had to make little (mulishly stubborn and tantrum-prone) children do it. Toys all over the place? Clean them up before the next toy gets taken out. Playdough all over the stairs? Scrape it up before we pull out the puzzles. Skeletal remains of a tea party all over the kitchen? Put it back before we have a real food snack. I've had more fat guppy lips and "No, Mamas!" tossed at me than I ever imagined, all the while the household staff (who loved my kids and would do anything not to let them be upset) edging in to start the clean up process. How in the world was I going to get my kids to learn how to be moderately self-reliant? A battle on so many fronts.

Now, I am thankful I made the unbelievably painful effort to teach my kids how to be moderately clean (about their toys; laundry is a different story). Actually, I look forward to giving my boys jobs; slave labor is highly underrated. With cleaners coming regularly, it's hard to enforce a household task. Now, I will be able to do so, and make sure that no one else is doing it for them. This is a simple pleasure of normal parenthood in the States, one that we miss out on overseas. I am going to really embrace these little chores for the boys, and I think they'll be better for it. Or at least their piggy banks will benefit from it.

That's not to say my kids don't like to help clean up. 'Help' clean up. When they add their assistance, it can take a full hour longer to accomplish a task. As we are cleaning (and talking, because little boys don't do anything without narrative), I am teaching them important skills and sharing quality time with them... says the good parent in me. All the while, bad parent is thinking *look at how filthy the floor still is! Honestly, just give me the broom and I'll do it myself!* Yet another battle on so many fronts. Since good parent will (hopefully) win, I usually end up re-cleaning the house the next day when the boys are at school or when they are asleep. There are only so many things I can stand stuck to the bottom of my feet.

I think what I need to do now is come to terms with just how neat the house should be, and how much time I want to devote to it. And weigh that against just how much filth, disarray, and general crap comes along with having four boys in the house (ages 2, 4, 6 and 40). This might just be the hardest part of not having a cleaner.

Susie Csorsz Brown is a Parent Coach, a trailing Foreign Service spouse (Niger, Tanzania, Cambodia, Burma, DC, unaccompanied Afghanistan), and a mom to three boys.

www.healthyexpatparent.com
Blog: www.duriandays.com/wordpress

Goodbye
Signe Hovem, American in Norway

A nod, a glance, a wink, a wave
a stubborn smile perchance.
A clasp, a hiss, a hug, a squeeze,
a delicate embrace.

But goodbye. Godspeed, toodleoo, adieu,
so long, farewell are simple words
too hard for me to say to you.

Let me depart without the parting words
(simple words are so simple you see —
they cut like swords —
their meanings too strong for all
their meaningless intentions:
the time and distance I try to ignore
lie opened and exposed —
slayed victims of the valedictions).

So take your leave with a nod a wave,
a hug a kiss, an enveloping embrace.
Or look me in the eye — even whisper your
well-wishes
But do not say the word 'goodbye'.

Signe Myers Hovem is a Colorado native, presently living in Baku, Azerbaijan. Married to a Norwegian, her four children have taught her first hand the cultural diversity and challenges of integrating two national identities. Her writing focuses on language as a spiritual tool, as means to promote self-awareness and authentic expression.

More **BOOKS** to make *you* feel *good* about life abroad

FROM

Summertime Publishing

AND AVAILABLE FROM

ExpatBookshop.com

Expat Life
Slice by Slice

APPLE GIDLEY

"An entertaining story, told with wit and insight"

Paul Burston, author, *The Gay Divorcee*

PERKING
THE PANSIES

Jack and Liam move to Turkey

JACK SCOTT

THE SINGING WARRIOR

FINDING HAPPINESS AFTER A PAST FILLED WITH PAIN

Niamh Ni Bhroin

BITTEN BY SPAIN

THE MURCIAN COUNTRYSIDE
⌐ A BAPTISM BY FIRE

DEBORAH FLETCHER

... had me chuckling from the first page till the last"

Vanessa Rocchetta, Expatica.com

The Thinking Tank

JAE DE WYLDE

'Sensitively written and delicately observed, an enthralling and suspenseful book that is literary but never difficult'
Leslie Ann Bosher, author, To The Manor Drawn

CPSIA information can be obtained at www.ICGtesting.com
Printed in the USA
BVOW071418050513

319850BV00001B/2/P